LINE BREAK

poetry as social practice

essays by
JAMES SCULLY

foreword by Adrienne Rich

Curbstone Press

Printed in the Unites States on acid-free paper by BookMobile
Cover design: Stone Graphics

"Remarks on Political Poetry" appeared in *The Poetry Society of America Bulletin* (LXXIV, 1983). "In Defense of Ideology" came out in a limited edition of *CCC* (Communist Committed Culture, #1, 1986). It was reprinted in *Fiction International* (18:1, 1998), where "Review: A Graphics Intervention in South Africa" also appeared (16:1, 1985). "Demagogy in the *Musée*" was published in *The Massachusetts Review* (XXVIII, 2, 1987), and "Scratching Surfaces: The Social Practice of Tendency Poetry" in *Minnesota Review* (n.s., 24, 1985). "Line Break" was commissioned for *The Line in Postmodern Poetry*, edited by Robert Frank and Henry Sayre (University of Illinois Press).

Library of Congress Cataloging-in-Publication Data

Scully, James.
Line break : poetry as social practice : essays / by James Scully.
    p. cm.
Originally published: Seattle, WA : Bay Press, c1988.
Includes bibliographical references.
ISBN 1-931896-18-6 (pbk. : alk. paper)
1. Political poetry—History and criticism. 2. Politics and literature. I. Title.
PN1081.S29 2004
809.1'9358—dc22
                                        2004029795

published by
  CURBSTONE PRESS   321 Jackson Street   Willimantic CT 06226
       phone: 860-423-5110   e-mail: info@curbstone.org
                        www.curbstone.org

Acknowledgements

Many people have been helpful, often without realizing it. Students have contributed much to this. I'm also indebted to Thatcher Bailey for his thoughtful editorial suggestions, to John D. Berry for his copy-editing and to Denise Abercrombie, Carrie Bramen, John Carey, Harold and Maggie Jaffe, Kurt Records, Jeff Schlanger, Alison Meyers's Everyday Books and the Ziesing Brothers bookstore. They are not responsible for what came of their interventions, questions and demurrals. The project began when Frank Reeve conceived a symposium on political poetry and Gardner McFall took the initiative to record my remarks and to have them transcribed.

For the current edition, Jane Blanshard's assiduous copy-editing of this recalcitrant text has been helpful.

Were it not for Adrienne Rich's openness and critical enthusiasm, *Line Break* would likely have remained out of print. I'm one of many who have reason to be grateful to her, directly and for the example she sets.

Note for the New Edition: Taking Poetry Seriously

Geopolitically and technologically, much has changed since these essays were written some 15-20 years ago. Upheavals on virtually every level have only made the aesthetic question less discrete, more implicated in just about everything, than it ever was supposed to be.

Line Break is best approached as though it were a quarry, or better yet "a heap of all that I could find"—as the Welsh poet David Jones (quoting Nennius) put it, apprehensive that certain crucial things, crucial values, might be "like smoke dissipated." There are no readymades here, no answers, just a lot of struggle with hard material. And challenges. The challenges *are* the point. The intention was not to write a polemic but to question aesthetic truisms: the fetishes we find ourselves wearing like ankle bracelets, alarms, that enable cultural overseers to shut us up in a kind of house arrest. To live with that is no way to live, nor to write. There's no future in it.

J.S. 2005

CONTENTS

FOREWORD

Poetry is neither an end in itself, nor a means to some external end. It's a human activity enmeshed with human existence; as James Scully names it, a social practice. Written where, when, how, by, for and to whomever, poetry dwells in a web of other social practices historically weighted with enormous imbalances of social power. To say this is not—as these essays vividly demonstrate—to deny the necessity for poetry as an art whose tangible medium is language.

It's a commonplace to say that in a society fraught with official lying, hyperbolic urgings to consume, contrived obsolescence of words (along with things and the people who produce them) poets must "recover" or "subvert" or "re-invent" language. Poetic language may thus get implicitly defined as autonomous terrain apart from the ripped-off or colonized languages of daily life.

It's an even older commonplace to claim "the imagination" as a kind of sacred turf. The appeal to a free-floating imagination permeates discussions of poetry and is traced to many honored sources from Coleridge to André Breton to Wallace Stevens to Barbara Guest. It can assume a degraded public world to which is opposed the poet's art as an activity-in-itself, distinct from other kinds of activity, work, production, save perhaps as metaphor.

Yet the imagination—the capacity to feel, see, what we aren't supposed to feel and see, find expressive forms where we're supposed to shut up—has meant survival and resistance, for poets and numberless others: incarcerated, under military or colonial occupation, in concentration camps, at grinding labor, suffering bleak and traumatic circumstances of many kinds. We may view the imagination as a kind of gated, landscaped neighborhood—or as a river, sometimes clogged and polluted, carrying many kinds of traffic including pollen and contraband, but in movement: the always-regenerating impulse toward an always-beginning future. Scully addresses the difference in his essay, "The Dream of an Apolitical Poetry," through the work of artists such as Gauguin, Woolf, Andrew Marvell, Mahmoud Darwish and Tadeusz Różewicz.

Most critical writing on poetry in the United States (I can't speak of elsewhere) has reached a pretty low point: degenerated into biographical juicy bits extracted from or imposed on poems, or "postmodern" self-referential jargon. Any poet whose work is both artistically searching and ideologically dissenting knows how shallow, therefore ultimately dismissive, even favorable critical response can be, isolating poems from their historical and social fields of energy—save perhaps as the poetry can be related to a recognized aesthetic movement. (But aesthetic movements, too, belong to historical and social processes and need critiquing in that light.)

This is a serious loss to poets (who might benefit from more informed and penetrating criticism); to readers (who might welcome discussion that could bring their reading of poetry into focus with a world which they know all too well to exist, could help them become the great readers Whitman declared a great poetry would need); and to the trajectory of all whose desire for social justice is inseparable from the need for beauty.

The imagination of an unrealized, humane social order is as passionate and ineluctable as the artist's search for unrealized expression. Scully puts the lie to the idea that one must preclude the other.

I found *Line Break* by chance on the Internet in 2002, searching for Scully's poetry. First published in 1988 by a small press in Seattle, it was out of print and already becoming unavailable. (Meanwhile, bookstores were stocked with manuals on poetry-writing as healing, as self-realization, as spiritual enlightenment—the commoditizing of some vague resource known as poetry, along with facile solutions to an unnamed general malaise.)

James Scully's essays, like his poems, refuse to soothe or simplify, to shortchange either poetry or the imperative for social revolution. They are continuously interesting because they take on poetry from so many angles, are written from a generous frame of reference and in a human voice. In the title essay Scully addresses the work that line-breaks actually do. Here questions of meter, free verse, punctuation and line interact with a discussion of liberalism and voice. In "Demagogy in the Musée" he unravels the assertions in Auden's celebrated "Musée des Beaux Arts," in terms of what is unmentioned in the poem. Elsewhere he lays open terms like "ideology," "protest poetry," "dissident poetry," and "poetic freedom." His fiercely demystifying intelligence is grounded in hope and realism for poetry in itself along with other forms of dissident engagement. It propels us into fertile argument with ourselves and others—Scully included.

Curbstone Press has long made possible books like this. It will be good news to many that *Line Break* is back in print. For new readers, in an apparently disconsolate time, it could be a window flung open, letting in necessary air and light.

Adrienne Rich, 2004

In *Letter to a Teacher* the peasant schoolboys of the Tuscan settlement of Barbiana—writing from a *doposcuola* for dropouts run by the village priest—criticize the public school system and the authorities who set the policies that downgrade, and expel, them and their kind. They fantasize that "if the poor would band together at the university, they could make a significant mark." But the few poor who do make their way into the university "are received like brothers by the rich and soon are rewarded with all their defects." What's more, "the men who staff the various political parties...are solidly university graduates. The proletarian parties are no different on this issue...There is a party bigger than all other parties: The Party of Italian College Graduates." The schoolboys conclude:

> When the new intermediate was being debated in Parliament, we, the mutes, kept silent because we were not there. The peasants of Italy were left out when a school for them was being planned.
> Eternal discussions went on between two factions, seemingly opposed to each other, but in fact the same.
> They were all graduates of the *liceo*, unable to see an inch beyond the school that had brought them to life. How could a young gentleman argue with his own shadow, spit on himself and on his own distorted culture while using the very words of that culture?[1]

Most of us have more in common with the schoolboys of Barbiana than we do with their failed teachers or their parliament, their talking society, of designated representatives. Currently, in the province of 'culture' we're overridden by poststructuralist theorists and postmodernist avant-gardes, regardless of political profession, speaking a uniformly muffled language behind one or another institutional wall. A wall that, though not opaque, is socially concrete—a scratchy, clouded distantiation like a sheet of old Lucite. Yet apart from the imagination and resources of mass political movement and organization, it's nearly impossible to break the constraints of institutional (en)closure. The historic attempt to pull down the monumental pieties of bourgeois humanism is entrusted to bright, respectable, silent butlers keeping the lid shut on social facts such as exploitation, class and race.

I realize that the almost inaccessible sites of theoretical and critical literary activity do not have much influence in the world at large. To imagine they do we'd have to slip into the idealist sinkhole of professors who believe that 'Classics' are "the books that shaped the western world." Nonetheless criticism and critical theory do have consequence—even if, sometimes, it is only as an oil-slick complacency ensuring that nothing happens in the back-and-forth slosh of what passes for culture.

It does not have to be that way. There is the healthier, productive "theory" described by Foucault when he was doing support work with prisoners: theory that is not simply consciousness-raising, and that "does not express, translate, or serve to apply practice: it is practice…This is a struggle against power, a struggle aimed at revealing and undermining power where it is most invisible and insidious. It is not 'to awaken consciousness' that we struggle…but to sap power, to take power; it is an activity conducted alongside those who struggle for power, and not their illumination from a safe distance."[2]

Victor Burgin has commented on the difference between "Matisse-inspired pictures" and a particular painting by Matisse.

[I was] struck by the difference in accomplishment between that Matisse and the 'new' Matisse-inspired pictures which filled the art magazines and galleries at that time—the latter were so much more successful. The Matisse itself was rather awkward. I had the impression of someone who did not quite *know* what they were doing, someone working 'at the edge' of what was possible and acceptable. Precisely what defines an *academy* is that it knows a success when it sees one, the criteria are already in place—success is then defined in terms of conformity to established criteria and *proficiency* in the execution of the exercise.[3]

We are reminded by this that there is no knowledge or accomplishment prior to, or apart from, practice. And practice entails awkwardness, working "at the edge."

Obviously the following essays have nothing in common with the Matisse except awkwardness and an inclination toward 'practice.' But like the schoolboys of Barbiana they too bear the scars of their making: race and gender conditioning, the odd emphases that come of working in a critically deflated environment, and vacillation regarding class position and outlook. Perhaps that goes with the territory. In any event my intention is not to summarize or settle but to reopen matters considered closed. In 1934 Walter Benjamin asked antifascist writers to produce and promote literature that is a means of production rather than an article of consumption, a literature that is a "compelling motive for decision" rather than "an object of comfortable contemplation." That still seems what is most worth doing. Aesthetic questions are political questions. It's tempting to add that aesthetic questions are political *in the last instance*, but that would only be a way of contemplating, and pretending to defer, the politic inscribed in them.

"Remarks on Political Poetry" is the edited transcript of an impromptu talk given to the Poetry Society of America at

NYU. In January 1983 the issue of political poetry was not taken as seriously, at least not in institutionalized cultural circles, as it is now. (The July-August 1987 issue of *The Women's Review of Books* transcribes the highly instructive speeches that June Jordan and Angela Davis delivered at a conference on "Poetry and Politics: Afro-American Poetry Today" which was held at Harvard University.) I had been scheduled to exchange views with Heberto Padilla, the Cuban exile poet, but he became ill and could not participate. I had learned of the manifesto cited in "Poetic Freedom and 'Cuba'" while preparing for that event. Later, anticipating an audience with different priorities, I wrote "The Dream of an Apolitical Poetry."

"In Defense of Ideology" began with a class on critical theory, but the piece was written at the request of a friend, a carpenter of communist principle, who insists on concepts that can be grasped and worked with.

"Demagogy in the *Musée*" circumnavigates Auden's "*Musée des Beaux Arts.*" It is based on a jargon-free demonstration, for an undergraduate class in literary criticism, of accessible approaches to literature. The project has less to do with the poem itself than with its status as a belletristic flagship.

"Scratching Surfaces: The Social Practice of Tendency Poetry" grew out of an attempt, soon abandoned, to write a blurb for two translated selections of Roque Dalton's poems. This led me to reconsider tendency writing and the bias against it—a bias shared by Marx and Engels as well as by most Anglo-American and western European poets and critics.

How to Commit Suicide in South Africa, the occasion for "Review: A Graphics Intervention in South Africa," is a neo-expressionist book featuring the iconography of gender oppression: a well-intentioned political enterprise whose graphics, overpowering the written text, transform a book on South African oppression into a vehicle for biologistic sexist/cultural presumption.

"Line Break" tests the possibility of articulating a poetic device as a social practice. The essay starts from Pierre Macherey's distinction between 'stylistics' and 'writing,' then goes on to analyze the unprescribed ("free") verse line break as untheorized punctuation with non-verse antecedents. Inasmuch as the essay was commissioned as a discussion, from the perspective of production, of the line in contemporary poetry, I conclude with examples from my own work.

1   Schoolboys of Barbiana, *Letter to a Teacher* (New York: Random House, 1970), 89-90.

2   Michel Foucault, *Language, Counter-Memory, Practice* (Ithaca, N.Y.: Cornell University Press, 1977), 208. Foucault charges that intellectuals "are agents of [the] system of power—the idea of their responsibility for 'consciousness' and discourse forms part of the system." Consequently "the intellectual's role is no longer to place himself 'somewhat ahead and to the side' in order to express the stifled truth of the collectivity; rather, it is to struggle against the forms of power that transform him into its object and instrument in the sphere of 'knowledge,' 'truth,' 'consciousness,' and 'discourse.'"

3   "The Absence of Presence: Conceptualism and Postmodernisms," *The End of Art Theory: Criticism and Postmodernity* (Atlantic Highlands, N.J.: Humanities Press International, 1986), 44-45.

REMARKS ON POLITICAL POETRY
excerpts from a talk

My first response to the symposium topic is to wonder what brings us to this pass, where we have a meeting about "politics and poetry." Not about kinds of politics, or kinds of poetry: just "politics" and "poetry." The issue, so defined, is so *un*defined it's quite crude. Not that we're to blame for this. It's remarkable that there even is such a meeting. Ordinarily "political poetry" is considered beneath comment. Nonetheless, if we look at the historical record, at the poetry that has been kept and revered, it's astounding that there are any reservations whatever about the viability of political poetry.

Of course there is a truth behind the assertion that poetry and politics don't mix, but one so warped it turns on itself. The truth is that much of what is called political poetry, or poetry that deals with politics, is hackwork. From this comes the generalization that politics destroys poetry. Yet isn't that an arbitrary conclusion? Most of *any* kind of poetry is hackwork, is slipshod, undemanding of itself. The work of idle hands that are maybe not idle enough. When you come upon an inept love poem you aren't likely to conclude that love and poetry don't mix. You may think the poet a bad poet, or even a callow person. And you may pass judgment on the work. But you won't jump to generalizations about the incompatibility of love and poetry.

There's a tendency to separate aesthetic quality and political poetry into mutually exclusive categories. Yet clearly anything we do has aesthetic quality (even wrapping a package: you do it well, or better, or poorly). Assertions that poetry and politics don't mix are not disinterested statements but political interventions in their own right. They presume not only that "poetry" and "politics" are autonomous categories, but also that there is such a thing as disinterested observation. Which is why, when one runs up against that particular pervasive bias, the result is seldom a discussion. There's nothing *to* discuss. Or so it's supposed to seem. In fact the attempt to dismiss, denigrate or suppress poetry that deals openly with political matters, or that has discomforting political implications, is just another version of the ongoing campaign—essentially a sociopolitical one—to determine what is or is not permissible in poetry. Not in poetry only, but in all expressive modes, from journalism through academic scholarship to cinema and pop music. (In one country the governing institutions call for "political" poetry. In another, the established consensus screens out all but "apolitical" poetry. Superficially they seem opposites, yet each has the same function: to block the mouth of poetry and/or cut off the view.)

Isn't it self-evident, as the Salvadoran poet Roque Dalton put it, that whatever fits into life fits into poetry? If we accept this in theory, why not in practice, where theory counts? Think what's at stake. Politics is not simply one more field or subject. The political dimension is not just another facet of life. It saturates and ramifies back into the most intimate areas of our lives, including whether we have jobs or don't have jobs, where we live or don't live, whether we have babies or don't have babies, and so on. We breathe it, we live it. It is more species-specific, more significantly human, than eating or sleeping or even procreation. How pretend that it doesn't exist or matter, or that it's off limits?

Earlier I made an analogy between political poetry and love poetry. In some respects that analogy, like any other, is misleading. Not all poetry is love poetry, but is there a poetry that is not political? An apolitical poetry? Well, yes and no. I mean, the very terms are up for grabs. There's poetry that's consciously political, and poetry that is unconsciously so; and either may be explicit or implicit in its politics. But the bottom line is that all poetry *is* political insofar as it bears a

2

set of assumptions about the organization and priorities of life, and carries with it a whole network of lives interpenetrating it, just as it interpenetrates life. Even its silences—sometimes especially the silences—have political content. As used ordinarily, however, "political poetry" is not applied to work that goes along with the ruling ideology of a given place or time. At the mention of "political poetry" no one is likely to think of Eliot, say, because his ideological coloration blends so well with that of the cultural stratum where his work is honored and preserved. The term "political poetry" is reserved for work that goes against the dominant ideological grain. It refers only to poetry that exhibits a certain *kind* of politics. Were we to use a more honest language, we might call this "dissident poetry," because that's what it is: the poetry of political dissidence.

By rights we should distinguish dissident poetry from protest poetry. Most protest poetry is conceptually shallow. I think of the typical protest anthology: poems in opposition to the Vietnam War or to the coup in Chile, ecologically concerned or antinuke poetry (with a few devastating exceptions, mainly Japanese), even poems sympathetic to workers (notably those that focus on workers' oppression, a symptomatic issue that leads to poetic moralizing while ignoring the exploitation that necessitates the oppression). Such poetry is issue-bound, spectatorial—rarely the function of an engaged artistic life, but compensation for a politically marginalized one. It tends to be reactive, victim-oriented, incapacitated, lacking the theoretical and practical coherence that could give it muscle and point. (Look at the *endings* of protest poems.) But the telltale characteristic of protest poetry is that it seldom speaks the active rage or resolution of people on the receiving end. I mean oppressed and exploited people. The real subject is the poet's own tender sensibilities, not what is actually, *systemically* going on. Dissident poetry, however, does not respect boundaries between private and public, self and other. In breaking

3

boundaries it breaks silences: speaking for, or at best *with*, the silenced; opening poetry up, putting it in the middle of life rather than shunting it off into a corner. It is a poetry that talks back, that would act as part of the world, not simply as a mirror of it. Obviously such a poetry rules nothing out. Dissident poetry does therefore observe connections—say, between social empowerment and valorization and human definition—that the dominant ideology declares that 'poetry' must ignore or suppress.

Most major poetry is consciously political, and always has been. Where do we want to start? With Aeschylus? Virgil? Dante? Can you imagine looking Dante in the face and saying poetry and politics don't mix? And these are 'canonized' poets: Milton, Blake, whoever. Do I have to mention Dryden? And then there are those "others"—like Spenser, whose reputation was made in one of the bigger con games in literary history. This is someone who's presented as a "pure" poet, a poet's poet! But when you look at what he wrote, and why, and at what he did, it's clear he was as consciously politicized as one may be. Aspects of those politics gave his language some regional grit, but mostly they were servile, vicious—in fact murderous. Yet, mean as they are, they still in some ways strengthen his writing (for instance, the political and career concerns that shadow and deepen the "Prothalamion"). Who's to say something similar doesn't hold true for poets such as Yeats—or Pound, whose politics were potentially more lethal? Or Akhmatova: an explicit political frame of reference made her work larger and more resonant than it had been.

Politically conscious poets tend to be *more* profound, not less. Look again at the record. In our own time the three most formidable poets, it seems to me, were intensely "political": the Turkish poet Nazim Hikmet, Vallejo and Brecht (as poet). Political in the most explicit, concrete, partisan way. What's more, their aesthetic achievement is *because of* their politics, not in spite of it. The most credible, full, caring love poetry has been written by one of the most expressly political poets. I refer, again, to Hikmet. In part this is because he can, and does, write of the *other*—who is never merely an excuse for self-immersion, and who is not reduced, either, to the condition of a delicious ahistorical object.

Finally, the propaganda that poetry and politics don't mix has served to trivialize both poetic and critical production. Not surprisingly it also tends to trivialize poetry that would break through the bubble of conventional ideology (ideology that justifies or abets the going relations of power). Such poetry is also shaped—formed and deformed, if you will— by the pressures of its time and place. Meanwhile, what has been lacking is not mindless detractors, of which there are many, but a serious, constructive, respectful criticism. A criticism mature enough to be self-effacing. Of course there is a critical industry of an abstracted sort—some of it nominally political—but it seems to have no basis in life *or* literature. In fact the current critical depression presents, or is symptomatic of, a serious problem facing *all* writers. The pressure to break poetry off into isolate fragments—to disarm it, cut it off—has made for a rather pathetic scene. As hegemonic political terms have lost institutional stability, coming unglued, our poetries and criticisms have not become more audacious, as might be expected, but distracted, withdrawn, diffident to the point of piety and arrogance. They have become mincers of words.

Ultimately this question has to be viewed in the context of the larger society: the entire web, a multilayered webbing, of social relations. What happens with so-called political poetry—how it is or is not received—does not depend on the literary world alone. But nothing else does either. This makes it only more shameful that in the literary context the response to dissent seems to be a wall of red-baiting or a wall of silence, but a wall in any case.

Just one thing I'd like to add: about the assumption that aesthetic limitations or disabilities are simply personal, or that one is personally responsible for them. There's a truth to that, surely, but a half-truth. The most decisive limitations on what we do or do not do, on how far we go or cannot go, are not essentially within us—they are historical, they're social, they surround us. Most cultural production is debilitated morally, humanly, aesthetically by the class and even caste system we must function in. No one transcends this. Yet that same system is a social creation, after all. It can and must be changed, for *aesthetic* as well as for other profoundly human reasons.

[*By way of conclusion I read a few poems. One concerned a friend of mine who is illiterate. The point was that his illiteracy stifles us, that without him—his access, his participation— whatever we write is disabled. The issue of poetries and criticisms cannot be considered apart from the social question.*]

IN DEFENSE OF IDEOLOGY

"Ideology" is becoming a socially degraded term. Wherever we turn, the guardians of cultural order are proscribing someone or something for being ideological—meaning, usually, that the offending party has a consistent, if not necessarily coherent, set of social and political ideas. Institutional intellectuals in particular seem intent on removing ideology from the realm of discussion. They manage this by reifying the *concept* of ideology. That is, by *lumping* it. Ideology goes on, but its degraded concept becomes a tar-and-feathers for certain classes of enemy who may be smeared, burned, with the epithet "ideological." In effect the bourgeois cultural apparatus tries to deny ideology by dehistoricizing it, by associating it with the perversion of ideas and "truth," and by dissociating it from the problematic and practice of power.

Ideology is indissociable from power: power as problematic, and power as practice. In the 1984 calendar put out by *Artists in Solidarity with the People of Central America,* the poster reproduced up front features the slogan:

NO MORE VIETNAMS

The poster shows a Vietnamese peasant woman in one landscape, a Central American campesino in another. Their two lands are united and overridden by a sky filled with U.S. helicopter gunships.

But on one copy of the calendar someone had blacked out the key word, "NO". The revised slogan read:

MORE VIETNAMS

This highlighted the 'subject position' of the original slogan, which had issued from a perspective of avoidance—specifically, avoidance of another costly, bloody, 'useless' war

---

7

in a country of no threat to the U.S. But as we know from the literature and songs of anti-imperialist struggles in Latin America and elsewhere (e.g., Victor Jara's *"El derecho de vivir en paz,"* or Che Guevara's call for "two, three, many Vietnams"), "Vietnams" are not necessarily to be avoided. For super-exploited peasants and workers in colonized areas, the Vietnam War is an inspiring example of resistance to imperialism. Unlike the *Artists in Solidarity,* revolutionary workers and campesinos of El Salvador would welcome another 'Vietnam,' meaning a victory over their foreign and domestic oppressors.

The North American pacifist, historically a bourgeois, wishes to abolish 'Vietnams.' All well and good. But if "No More Vietnams" means 'No More Vietnam Wars,' it does *not* mean 'no more colonies of systemic oppression and super-exploitation.' For that, the slogan would have to admit means by which 'Vietnams' (colonies of super-exploitation, not the struggles against them) might be eliminated. "No More Vietnams," morally attractive though it is, is a *class* slogan: a slogan of those who can afford to have nothing happen. Or of those who, under the sway of bourgeois ideological hegemony, against their better interests *think* they can afford to have nothing happen. But it is *also* a slogan of those who openly wish to maintain those colonies—who say "No More Vietnams" in the same breath as they say "No More Cubas." In fact they actively link the two sayings. As Randolph Ryan noted in the *Boston Globe,* foreign policy militants in the Reagan administration promise "'No more Cubas, but also no Vietnams.'" As Ryan explains this historical invocation, "it is central to their premise of tidy 'low intensity' wars that the Sandinistas can be felled without U.S. ground forces." But not everyone shares this view or these values. Nor is the option available to all. That is why the revolutionary Central American campesino, unlike the middle-class North American pacifist, wishes to reproduce the successful struggle of 'Vietnam.' To her or him, 'Vietnam' is resistance, the process

> by which people who are objects become subjects. Become, in a word, people. For them, 'Vietnam' does not, as it must for much of the bourgeois and campus left of the U.S., stand for bloody futility.

We have compelling reason to rehistoricize and socially resituate the concept of ideology, restoring it as an instrument of liberation. The alternative, which is no alternative at all, is to let it be conscripted by social silence and reaction.

the concept as a site of struggle

The concept of ideology is itself a site of ideological struggle. Here and now that site is appropriated and reappropriated, furiously domesticated, by the bourgeoisie and its cultural functionaries. Their obfuscation of it is a tactic in what Gramsci called "the war of position," the struggle to overturn, or to maintain, the ideological hegemony exercised by any ruling class (regardless of composition, and regardless of what metaphysical taxonomy that class conforms to or confounds) over the social formation as a whole. A war, we might add, conducted with comparable intensity in fields of race, gender and nation.

A generalized, ahistorical concept of ideology only reinstates critical unconsciousness. It is itself ideological, helping to maintain the status quo while appearing not to do so. A historically situated concept, however, may be counter-hegemonic. It need not be an instrument of suppression.[1]

the bourgeois (ideological) definition of ideology

Any capitalist system, no matter how sophisticated or crude, must turn what it touches into a commodity. Goods, tools, artworks and people are dehistoricized, stripped of human significance and shrouded in parody value ('exchange value').

Rather than being constituted as subjects, they are laid out as historical objects. They become the debris of history, not a compelling motive informing it. People are purged of humanity, but so too are goods, institutions, ways of being born and making love and dying...as are 'intangibles,' concepts, including the concept of ideology.

Active and passive defenders of the status quo define ideology as bad or false political ideas. Yet they aren't the only ones to do so. Many leftists resent the *application* of this definition, especially as it is used against them. Nonetheless they go along with the definition itself, accepting "ideology" as meaning ideas that are clung to irrationally, superstitiously, like an amulet against the evil eye. To be ideological is to be dogmatic, numbskulled, willful. Eventually their fear of being labeled "ideological" slides over into a fear of ideas as such, especially ideas that demand enactment.

The ramifications are not always amusing. Anti-intellectual leftists may brandish the dis-articulated epithet "ideological" in the same way, for the same reason, that bourgeois rightists and liberals do—to dismiss communist ideas without having to contend with them. Slogans appealing to "workers" may be tagged and rejected as "ideological." Yet "worker" is a material, socially locatable category. At the very least a worker (occupational *forms* aside) is anyone who must live by the sale of his or her labor power, and who has no other life-sustaining resources. Yet those same leftists may direct their own slogans to "the people," though "the people" is an immaterial category used opportunistically, which is to say demagogically, by everyone from the KKK to the president to rightist and leftist protest groups. They conceive "the people" as a loose baggy monster, albeit a benign one. It may be plumped up with anything, with all kinds of indigestible contradictions crammed into it. The terrible thing is, under this evasive, stubborn, obfuscating regime *any* attempt at definition can only degenerate into a kind of mud-wrestling...into the head-butting, sectarian arrogance that keeps the bourgeois left churning in place. A place, we might add, assigned to it by this wonderful system of exploitation with its fringe, its scattering fringe, of symbolic opposition.

The fundamental problem is this: a concept of ideology that reduces "ideology" to a metahistorical category of damnation may reinforce or stigmatize beliefs *but it cannot critique them.* Under it, empowered social values are unlikely to be considered ideological, whereas systemically subversive values assuredly will be. Yet the determination of what is or is not politically bad or false, or dogmatic, or "ideological," is power. Truth doesn't separate the non-ideological sheep from the ideological goats—power does.

The word "ideological" is itself a bone of contention, but one appropriated by the powerful *regardless* of any relation or non-relation to 'truth.' Ordinarily the epithet is used— *empowered*—in the way the word 'terrorist' is. Under the Reagan government, terrorists who murder innocent people in airports are terrorists, whereas U.S. mercenaries *(contras)* who murder innocent people in Nicaragua are 'freedom fighters.' Chinese or Rumanian tennis players and Russian ballet dancers enter the U.S. as 'refugees,' but Salvadoran women bearing marks of torture must be 'illegal aliens.' A Haitian doctor is branded an 'illegal alien,' though a Ukrainian illegal alien is a 'defector,' and the tens of thousands of illegal Irish immigrants in Boston and New York are none of the above because it has been quietly determined by media and immigration officials that they shall melt into the landscape. Who gets what designation is determined by those who have the social and political power *to* designate.

Bourgeois-conceived 'ideology' is not simply a rough-and-ready political weapon, but an obliterating presence. It blocks out whatever troubles the self-serving, colorless, odorless assumptions and values with which one class or group exercises hegemony over society as a whole.[2]

the bourgeois conceives 'ideology' as AN ideology,
a demythified myth

Any dominant power (whether materialized as class, race, gender or nation) has a vested interest in defining ideology the way schools define myth: as a visible body of beliefs held by somebody else, somewhere else, possibly a long time ago. Yet such 'myth' is like the propaganda that Jacques Ellul calls "a paper tiger." Manageable, distanced, isolable, it has no cutting edge, no power to slip past one's guard. It may have affect, but it effects nothing. The bourgeois notion of ideology is comparable to demythified myth. No need to stop the ears or lash ourselves to the mast. It cannot get to us. We are *proof* against it.

but ideology is like myth itself

Effective myth is historicized. Myth is myth only for those suffused with it. Historically constituted, having no existence of its own, myth is inseparable from life lived. That is why mythic relations are experienced as literal relations. Myth is the very condition of thought, not thought's object.

The same is true of ideology, which is more problematical in that we must still struggle to theorize it. Ideology is the most pervasive, intense cultural policing we are subjected to. What security agency or police force can compare with it? We may absorb other kinds of losses, but the battle against ideology is one we cannot afford to lose.

what is ideology?

No matter how it is used, the term "ideology" has a critical cast. It is value-laden. The thing is, an undefined 'ideology' is itself ideological, whereas a socially situated, historically specific concept of ideology is anti-ideological, and necessarily so.

What then are the qualifications of ideology, of a *concept* of ideology, that may be used against ideology itself?

1) *Ideology involves misrepresentation and/or misrecognition.* As Louis Althusser puts it, "ideology is a representation of the imaginary relationship of individuals to their real conditions of existence."

Ideology may be "false consciousness," a misunderstanding of what is going on and *why*, but it is not only that. False consciousness *is* consciousness, a personal and social fact. (The notion of a "false consciousness" is provisional, a shorthand convenience. In the long run it would be misleading to speak of a 'false' consciousness, as that implies a 'true' consciousness, or consciousness of *the* truth. There is, and is not, a true or a false consciousness. What there is, is a historically and socially conditioned consciousness whose truth or falsity depends on its correspondence to the actual conditions of one's life). In fact, ideology entails the misunderstanding of our relationship to what goes on, socially, *even as* it conditions that relationship. It is not simply something we manipulate or are manipulated by.

Ideological conditioning so 'places' us that we misrecognize ourselves. The ideological conditioning we're most subject to, that of bourgeois humanism, encourages us to imagine that we're transcendental subjects—indivisible, ahistorical entities—rather than socially, historically constituted subjects. Yet each of us is a nexus of social relations. Not merely 'is affected by,' but *is* those relations. The more we take account of that—in practice and not just in contemplation, the 'freer' we may be. Conversely, the more we conceive ourselves as autonomous, self-generated subjects, the more we become functions of our systemic environment. Lacking the critical consciousness to engage in social *practice,* we remain social functionaries. We become (functions of) the system, the standing organization and distribution of power.

2) *Ideology is transparent.* It is *lived* misunderstanding: as indissociable, disarming and self-evident as common sense. It is not, as the bourgeoisie would have it, a book or a batch of transcendent, detachable ideas. Ideology does not consist in the advocacy of ideas. Rather, it informs talking, writing, thinking, working, making love, dreaming, raising kids. It is inscribed in the way we do these things and in the very language that substantiates the discourses of law, physics, TV sitcoms, education theory, bohemian culture, medical procedures, etc.

According to Raymond Williams in *Writing in Society,* ideology is, in effect, "the condition of all conscious life. Thus the area to which most students of literature normally refer their reading and their judgment, that area summarized in the decisive term 'experience,' has in fact to be seen as the most common form of ideology. It is where the deep structures of the society actually reproduce themselves."

3) *Ideology confirms and extends existing power* (power meaning power *over*). We might define ideology as integration propaganda (as opposed to agitation propaganda—which is denigrated offhandedly, ideologically, as "agitprop"). Agitation propaganda is a systemically oppositional practice. Integration propaganda, though, would deepen our incorporation in a socially empowered system, whatever that system may be. It would make us functionaries of the system. Integration propaganda, then, is an exercise in political hegemony. It is the pervasive propaganda that would absorb us, the propaganda whose very language is intended to impose silence.[3] As that propaganda succeeds, we lose the power of speech. *It* speaks *us.* We may mouth words, but the mouthing of words does

not alone qualify as speech. Insofar as we are functions of ideology, of systemic integration propaganda, our talk is only so much silence. Social silence.

In turn, our silence is our overrulers' power, and ideology is their Great Facilitator. Through ideology the existing social formation—which is little more than the inequitable distribution of power as it has been legalized, mediated and 'naturalized' in the form of a complex system—reproduces itself and its relations of production "by producing people, not just biologically but socially, and not just in terms of skills but of attitudes" (Antony Easthope, *Poetry as Discourse*). In a sense, ideology is the dream work of capitalism. People too may be a kind of latent content, a raw material. Capitalist ideology is constantly working to "create" people in its own image.

4) *Ideology naturalizes itself.* The most powerful function of ideology is not to obfuscate or mask, but to disarm: to insinuate that what is, is. And to prevent the recognition that what is, is becoming—is becoming not because of some 'external' agency, a god out of the machine, but because internal contradiction generates instability, movement and change (without, however, definitively directing that change).[4] The fact is, everything is riddled with contradiction. Ideology smoothes over, harmonizes, so that all appears seamless, unanalyzable, inalterable.

The assumptions and values of any ruling class or caste (as Marx and Engels so trenchantly put it) are the prevailing ones: "The class which is the ruling *material* force of society is at the same time its ruling *intellectual* force...Their [assumptions] take on the form of universality" (*The German Ideology*). Those assumptions and values no longer appear to be socially situated or historically conditioned. They seem rooted in the natural order, in tune with the way things are. Nonetheless, they're in keeping only with the way things happen to be at a certain time in a certain place. There is nothing natural or universal about either the assumptions or the values. They correspond to the prevailing social order (the organization of power).

The bottom line is roughly this: ideology, which has so much to do with the control, shaping and legitimation of knowledge and 'truth,' in the last instance is not about knowledge at all. What it's 'about' is power, social power. Ideologies are "mobilizations within the class struggle" (Terry Lovell, *Pictures of Reality: Aesthetics, Politics and Pleasure*). That is how they are to be understood, and how they must be judged.

ideology at work

Recently President Reagan claimed that the government of South Africa had largely eliminated segregation by integrating hotels, restaurants and other facilities. His lie was characterized by some critics as "ideological." That is, what he had said was untrue, but he needed to believe it, and have us believe it, in order to justify his "constructive engagement" (support) of the South African government. Yet though he did misrepresent the reality, and glibly skimmed over an abyss of contradiction—still, this was not ideology. His pronouncement effectively underwrote the South African hierarchy, one which he rightly feels interlocks with the U.S. hierarchy that he himself represents and serves, but that pronouncement was not transparent. It was opaque, a clunker, having congealed its political project. We could see it, question it, evaluate it.

At about the same time, a seemingly nonpartisan headline appeared on the cover of *U.S. News and World Report:*

CAN SOUTH AFRICA AVOID RACE WAR?

Posed as a question, the headline was nonetheless an ideological intervention. It placed itself and us in a certain subject position vis-à-vis the struggle consuming South Africa. We were *sided* with the South African ruling race and class.

For all groups except genocidal organizations—the Christian Identity movement, the Kach Party and the like— "race war" is coded negative. Hardly anyone anywhere wants a race war. Because "race war" is undesirable, the headline effects a positive communication. It characterizes the present South African situation as one that is free of race war. And that is a good thing.

Or is it? There is, after all, a catch. It holds out the hope that South Africa may possibly avoid race war, *but what is apartheid?* Isn't South Africa organized according to the apartheid system, and isn't apartheid itself a race war? More a "war of position" than a war of movement, but war nonetheless. And isn't apartheid a war on behalf of one race against others? A war *in the name of* one race against those *designated* "others"?[5] What's more, isn't apartheid, to get down to it, not the recognition but the construction of races, without which there would be no basis for race war? (This is fairly easy to see, because apartheid's racist constructions do not always coincide with our own. U.S. publications stumble over the category of Coloureds, often dissociating themselves from it by means of inverted commas, much as they would if handed the now-discredited categories—discredited even in racist terms—of mulatto, quadroon or octaroon.) Yet that is only the bare bones of the matter.

CAN SOUTH AFRICA AVOID RACE WAR?

The headline purges its form of content. (It fissures, leaving a 'form' and a 'content': the form of the headline goes back on what it seemed to promise, delivering instead a contradictory 'content.') The state of South Africa is emptied of its substance as apartheid; that is, as a state of race war. But the headline also dislocates the prevailing state of affairs (South African apartheid) by resituating it in the nonwar, 'peaceful,' eye of the storm swirling about it. There it sits, the calm center, threatened by the cataclysmic extremism called "race war."

But how can "South Africa," now recognizable as the code name for apartheid, for institutionalized race war, be threatened by race war?

> CAN SOUTH AFRICA AVOID RACE WAR
>
> APARTHEID
>
> RACE WAR

The institutionalized race war that is called "South Africa" can be so threatened, because what the headline calls "race war" is a code term for *resistance to race war*. As ideological transposition has turned the apartheid race war into "South Africa," it has turned the struggle against that race war into "race war." This sleight of terms has not simply obscured a reality or made it disappear—it has turned reality inside out, so that what is said is what is not, while what is not is what is set forth.

> CAN SOUTH AFRICA <u>AVOID</u> RACE WAR?
>
> APARTHEID   RESISTANCE TO RACE WAR
>
> RACE WAR

The most transparent word may be the most subtly ideological. The predication "avoid" is not only anti-dialectical (reductively mechanical) in its assumptions—it is anti-practice and anti-struggle. What's given, as though beyond question, is that it is positively blessed to avoid. "Avoid" is coded positive as "race war" is negative. Yet Avoidance, we realize, sits ever at the right hand of Status Quo. And that is the point. The status quo (the state as *quo*) is what avoidance serves.[6]

Through "avoid," South Africa is presented as a self-acting entity: an irreducible *being* without internal contradiction, without struggle, without articulate historical constituency. A being without becoming. A transcendental subject that

18

happens to find itself in a troubling historical *situation*. But what is the human constitution of this transcendental subject? If "race war" is the code term for resistance to race war, what is the racial composition of the South Africa that wants to avoid such resistance? (Keep in mind, though we cannot here attend to the fact, that what has been historically produced is not only the "racial composition" of South Africa, but the 'races' that are its ingredients.)

The headlined "South Africa," we've noted, encodes the apartheid-constituted South African government. "South Africa" is the name for what suppresses the human existence of the majority population of South Africa. From that majority it admits only the likes of Chief Buthelezi, the Inkatha goon squads, police and political collaborators.[7] The headline not only takes over the majority, the resisters of race war, and defines them out of South Africa, thereby creating a mythical "South Africa"; it appropriates their historical meaning, reassigning it to the administrators of institutionalized race war. So race war is peace, and resistance to it is war or the threat of "race war." What is, isn't; what isn't, is.

Orwell didn't know half as much about newspeak as the editors of the *U.S. News and World Report* do. Their headline, which has the feel of a concerned question, is not a question but a position. Note too that the question isn't posed in terms of prediction or foreknowledge. It does not ask *will* South Africa avoid race war, but *can* it. The predication presupposes an empathetic relationship to "South Africa." As with the little engine that could—huffing and puffing uphill, gritting it out, saying, "I think I can, I think I can"—the *can* ushers us into kinesthetic identification with "South Africa." We are *with* it. Our muscles and nerves, our reflexes if not our hearts, go out to it. The headline, then, surfaces from the subject-position of the besieged racist government of South Africa. It's just one more version of the banner raised over the Afrikaner *laager*. It signals the last-ditch racist position: to be holed up, with no relief in sight, holding off the endlessly encircling hordes. As a social practice,

> CAN SOUTH AFRICA AVOID RACE WAR?

means

> CAN SOUTH AFRICAN APARTHEID AVOID
> (can we, with it, avoid)
> THE STRUGGLE AGAINST APARTHEID?

Although the *U.S. News and World Report* headline does not openly state a set of social values, *it does occupy a socially specific position.* As ideology it makes a subject-position for us under its wing—the while brooding on, and generating, the values *of* that position. We live out those values insofar as we fail to develop critical consciousness of that position, or insofar as we mistake the headline for a question, failing to comprehend it as a position. Finally, the headline intervenes on behalf of the dominant power. It supports the continuation of the South African apartheid government. What worries that government is what worries *U.S. News and World Report.* They are brothers under the skin.

The casual bourgeois definition of ideology would make us incapable of *articulating* ideology. Not that bourgeoisified 'ideology,' meaning bad or false political beliefs, is a useless concept. It is quite useful for those who wish to turn the concept of ideology into a dead letter. Or who would apply the term, as an epithet, only to disempowered and hence discredited ideas. Or who would use it as a rail on which to ride those ideas out of town. But for this reason it is in our interest to defend and enact a technical, socially and historically specific concept of ideology. Without a concept of ideology, we cannot critique it.

1   The dehistoricized *concept* is a site of struggle. As that concept/site is historically situated and appropriated, however, it becomes a revolutionary or reactive agency.

2   The notion of "society as a whole," which assumes a noncontradictory identity, is itself a function of ideology. Althusser uses the more critical, less organicist "social formation" rather than "society." The social formation is a site of contradiction and struggle.

3   The deepest silence may be produced by criticism itself. That is, ideologized criticism within a system may be the most effective confirmation *of* that system. As Noam Chomsky notes, "It is necessary to control not only what people do, but also what they think...Thought can lead to action and therefore the threat to order must be excised at the source. It is necessary to establish a framework for possible thought that is constrained within the principles of the State religion. These need not be asserted; it is better that they be presupposed, as the unstated framework for thinkable thought. The critics reinforce this system by tacitly accepting these doctrines and confining their critique to tactical questions that arise within them. To achieve respectability, to be admitted to the debate, they must accept without question or inquiry the fundamental doctrine that the State is benevolent, governed by the loftiest intentions...The more intensely the debate rages between hawks and doves [over the war in Vietnam], the more firmly and effectively the doctrines of the State religion are established. It is because of their notable contribution to thought control that the critics are tolerated, indeed honored—that is, those who play by the rules..." Noam Chomsky, "The Manufacture of Consent," *Our Generation* 17:1 (Fall/Winter 1985-86), 100-101.

4   Logically, contemplatively, contradiction leads to impasse. Historically, contradiction generates instability, movement, revision. Contradictory elements may be 'perfectly' balanced in mind, in abstraction, but not in life.

5   The South African government would protest that apartheid is not race war—that, on the contrary, it is the sole guarantee of racial harmony. Without racial separation, they claim, there would be racial and tribal conflict. As proof they point to hostilities such as those presently flaring up between Zulus and Pondos. Yet the argument is disingenuous. That conflict is a direct result of apartheid and of the move to assign people to so-called homelands, bantustans (juridical slums or ghettos with names and flags and not much else), on the basis of reimposed tribal affiliations. The recent fighting was provoked by the South African government, which had taken land from one group and awarded it to another. What's more, if separation of hostile 'races' were the South African government's motive, there would be

no need to provoke further conflict by articulating separation as a hierarchy: whites ruling over all, and the rest subdivided into a layer of Asians and 'Coloureds' on top of a vast substratum of blacks. But then racial harmony is not, and never was, the project of that government. In the interests of domination and exploitation, racial harmony is precisely what apartheid was designed to avoid.

6 Even in a potentially oppositional headline, e.g., CAN U.S. AVOID NUCLEAR WAR?, "avoid" produces its own despiteful intent. What it intends, *effectively*, is to avoid contention with what must be contended with. The headline is locked into a symptomatic mode. The terms of the question preempt the possibility of solution. But substantively, which is to say historically, 'avoidance' would have to be enacted as non-avoidance. The *words* for actualized avoidance would be words of confrontation, contention, struggle. Unlike the headline, a non-ideological question would ask whether war organizations may be disbanded. Whether exploitation, the profit system that fuels and thrives on the machinery of war, may be done away with. To avoid nuclear war is not to avoid nuclear war but to take on all this; is not to adopt a high ground, but to negate the systemic necessity of war. Not to be a morally superior witness, but to be a destroyer of that system and its criminal necessities.

Of course this doesn't account for the discrepancy between what "U.S." supposedly represents and what its specific historical composition is. ("U.S." bears on the territory and population of the U.S. pretty much as the headlined "South Africa" does on the territory and population of South Africa.) Nor does this discussion acknowledge that the historical U.S., unlike the mythical "U.S." of the headline, is a generative component of nuclear war, and not easily, if at all, distinguishable from it.

7 The situation is complicated, though not substantially altered, by the fact that at least two unions, the Council of Unions of South Africa and the Azanian Confederation of Trade Unions, are black nationalist. They will neither admit white workers nor ally with unions that do.

Recently the South African government has refrained from attacking the "Black Consciousness" movement, having given a free hand to Buthelezi and Inkatha. That's because, along with the South African government, they too perpetrate race and 'tribal' war. Being concerned mainly to get a larger slice of the pie, Inkatha does not take on apartheid racism (except through a few of Buthelezi's generalized pieties), but does carry out vicious attacks, including assassinations, against members of the multiracial United Democratic Front (UDF).

DEMAGOGY IN THE *MUSÉE*

About suffering they were never wrong,
The Old Masters: how well they understood
Its human position...

1

By now, we suppose, Auden too is an Old Master—if not of the human position then of the humanist one. His conception of the human, presented as universal and given, is of course historically specific and problematic. For this reason and others we might not revere his instruction. The Old Master is also the Old Craftsman, for whom philosophies were conveniences, racks for hanging poems on. Auden, in the allegory of his progress, passed through Marxism, Freudianism, and Existential Christianity before settling into Domesticity in a suburb of Vienna. Even his admirers have had trouble taking this junkyard of capital letters seriously. Auden too seems to have been ambivalent about them. Crass concepts lie scattered about like ideas from a musical comedy, an embarrassment that many would prefer to ignore. But except for his last phase, which yielded little of either, Auden provided less wisdom than entertainment anyway. Ideas were the sugar coating on what was really of moment in his poetry—virtuoso sensuousness and a consonant, vowelish charm. *Summer, water, saunter.*

Yet if Auden wore his beliefs lightly, they were nonetheless there. In December 1938, in the backwash of his *engaged* phase, unable to shake a nagging social consciousness, he wrote "*Musée des Beaux Arts.*"

About suffering they were never wrong,
The Old Masters: how well they understood
Its human position; how it takes place
While someone else is eating or opening a window or just walking
        dully along;
How, when the aged are reverently, passionately waiting
For the miraculous birth, there always must be
Children who did not specially want it to happen, skating
On a pond at the edge of the wood:
They never forgot
That even the dreadful martyrdom must run its course
Anyhow in a corner, some untidy spot
Where the dogs go on with their doggy life and the torturer's horse
Scratches its innocent behind on a tree.

In Brueghel's *Icarus*, for instance: how everything turns away
Quite leisurely from the disaster; the ploughman may
Have heard the splash, the forsaken cry,
But for him it was not an important failure; the sun shone
As it had to on the white legs disappearing into the green
Water; and the expensive delicate ship that must have seen
Something amazing, a boy falling out of the sky,
Had somewhere to get to and sailed calmly on.

Though the homely goings-on may beguile us, this homily on a 16th-century painting is framed as effectively as a slide of skin tissue in a lab. Auden's report on the significance of a 400-year-old painting is not a report, really, but the reappropriation of a dehistoricized configuration. The poem's "painting" is Auden's, not Brueghel's. Even when painting and poem details seem the same, they are not. They are coded differently. They depend on different exclusions. What in the painting bespeaks a positive relationship to daily life, in the poem promotes disengagement. Brueghel's painting may be a document of intellectual history, or the symptom of a phase in that history. But in the poem any and all history, including the poem's own contemporaneity, is blotted out. Or almost blotted out. To enter the *Musée* one must undergo a desperately selective amnesia.

The *Musée* has one obvious structural feature: it is sustained by dyadic formulations. These are not peculiar to this poem but are typical of Auden's work. His eminently packageable assurance depends upon a preemptive habit of thinking only in terms of paired units: the Virgin and the Dynamo, Quixote and Panza, Rome and Monticello, Hic et Ille, Alices and Mabels, etc. In the *Musée* the dyad is openly hierarchical. Although presented in different forms, it is most often expressed as empathy and 'other' awareness versus ignorance and self-absorption. The catch is that the *Musée*'s rankings project social values that seem to contradict received ones. The peripheral is central, and the momentous is relegated to the margins where, in the scheme of *actual* human valuing, it is declared to belong. Suffering is remote, or experienced as negligible, whereas eating, opening a window, or "just walking dully along" are sited in the midst of human life. In the logic of the *Musée*, the marginal that is central should be central, and the momentous that is pushed into the background should be put there. Everything gets the significance it deserves. Children skating on a pond "at the edge of the wood" have true human perspective. Their indifference occupies the foreground of the poem and substantiates the understanding of the Old Masters. The Old Masters, who make nothing happen, report what does, and what does is a lot of coming and going, mostly going. The *Musée* is not unlike a railway station or an apartment building fallen into anomie. It is a site of leaving, of turning away and getting away.

The emblem of this 'vision of reality' is Brueghel's *Landscape with the Fall of Icarus* (1558). In it the legendary Icarus plunging into the sea becomes an anonymous boy, or less—a pair of splayed, discombobulated legs about to follow their body crashing into the water. (The poem, less lighthearted, transforms these into aestheticized "white legs" disappearing into "green / Water.") The centerpiece of the painting, its declaration of perspective and value, is the ploughman doing contour ploughing. He, the ship and the rest confirm that life goes on. Missing from the poem are the fisherman sitting on the bank, evidently not noticing, and the shepherd with his dog and sheep. The shepherd is as much the butt of Brueghel's humor as Icarus is. He's standing, peering up into the sky—but in the wrong direction. What he may be looking for, what has already dropped out of the sky, is splashing into the harbor behind him. Brueghel's benignly critical realism cuts both ways: in its wry, cracker-barrel perspective, the legendary and the mundane are equally amusing. Yet that evenhandedness may not be the only reason why the shepherd and the fisherman were banished from the *Musée*. It's not simply that the painting is less than reverent toward the mundane, which in the poem is fetishized as the measure of human truth and value, but that the very categories "shepherd" and "fisherman" raise *social* implications that the poem must put out of mind. It's one thing to raise the spectre of "miraculous birth" or "dreadful martyrdom," but quite another to evoke the shepherd, whose job is to care for his flock—or even, though this is more tenuous, the fisher of men. Why this is so should become clear as we spend time in and around the *Musée*. Suffice it to say that Brueghel's painting is affirmative as the poem is not. Even the obscured head of an old man, presumably dead, lying in the thicket under a tree, is neither tragic nor ghoulish. Like fallen fruit, the death is part of life. Life goes on as it does, not out of cynicism or selfishness but because it is bumbling, imperfect, and positive. The ploughman is ploughing up ground, or rather, furrowing the earth. In general, the brightly colored painting, a yellow sun on the horizon of its bay, shrugs off myth as if it were old dead skin. It's *Spring*! with a vengeance. The awkward legs of Icarus might be those of a kid hurling himself with springtime abandon, headfirst into the water.

But that's Brueghel's painting. In the *Musée* the turning away is deliberate, a denial rather than an affirmation. Brueghel's painting is a landscape with figures, whereas Auden's work disposes figures in a social void. There is no ground, no 'glue.' The absence of connections corresponds to the denial of interaction, a denial that anything effectively happens. Significantly, the *Musée*'s children do not specially want "it" or anything to happen. The superiority of the Old Masters is their understanding that nothing *does* happen (nothing alters, in any way whatever, the given order). What does not happen, which is to say what is not unnatural, prevails. At the same time this ahistorical tableau features a compensatory array of empirical, pseudoconcrete movements. Everyday is preoccupied with the hum and humdrum of life—eating, opening a window, walking, skating, going on, scratching, turning away, sailing on. With so much referenced activity we may not notice that nothing happens in the *Musée*. The "miraculous birth," a historical rupture of the natural (given) order, does not come about. Nor does its consequence, the "dreadful martyrdom" that like a disease "must run its course." Nor does the ship that "sailed calmly on." Having been plotted, having "somewhere to get to," it too must run its prescribed course.

The inversion of certain received values does not necessarily challenge the hierarchical system. True, those values may be unsettled by the implication that the passionate, irrational, waiting elders are less knowledgeable than the skating children. The automatic indifference of the children gives *them* the proper perspective. Yet the traditional hierarchical structure is reconfirmed: the instinctive wisdom (ignorance) of the skating children gives them, in their unconsciousness, the wisdom the Old Masters consciously have. A presumed hierarchy (the conscious old are wiser than the unconscious young) has been rattled only to be reinstated (the intuitive 'knowledge' of the skating children is absorbed and elevated into the understanding of the *Old* Masters). This in turn confirms another received value: that seers have it over doers. Only the Old Masters have the capacity for thought. The rest are hands, feet, mouth, rump. In the *Musée*, authority resides with the Old Masters, who reflect; not with Icarus, who leaps before he thinks.

The Old Masters, who see and know, are set over against Icarus, who is seen and known. Perspective is not centered in the ploughman or in someone just eating, or in any one or thing whose indifference or ignorance constitutes the Old Masters' understanding, but in the Old Masters themselves, who preside over these simple incorporators of wisdom, the plain folk, the way an eagle sits at the top of a food chain. It is one of the many curious dislocations of the *Musée* that in it the bearers and producers of understanding do not *have* that understanding. The ploughman, the skating children and the rest only produce the understanding that gives substance to the Old Masters, who appropriate and *realize* that understanding—who make it their own, as Auden makes the 'understanding' of the Old Masters *his* own.

These and other dyadic formulations only confirm the order of slice-of-life commonsense, of empirical perception and value. But to what end? Why confirm that order? We know that the commonplace not only occupies the foreground but is thrust into it—so that the torturer's horse's behind looms larger than the torture, whereas the extraordinary and the morally critical are crowded out of the picture. Again, why? We may wonder if the *Musée* isn't in response to a social imperative—one similar to that elaborated in the parable of the Good Samaritan. There must be no shepherds, no suggestion of shepherds, in this *Musée*. No watching over, nor watching out for. Is the Old Masters' understanding their understanding that the *Musée* does not accommodate those who do *not* turn away? Is the world of the *Musée*, the avuncular tone notwithstanding, basically antisocial?

What's going on is not evasion, exactly, but crisis

management. In its studiously casual yet relentless way the *Musée* diminishes, occasionally demeans, whatever is potentially transformative or morally/philosophically compelling. It promotes what Yeats's "Lapis Lazuli" declaimed (published March 1938, six months before *Musée* was written) with praise of unmoved tragic actors and of ancient Chinese musician/sages on their mountainside—playing mournful melodies, but with gay, glittering eyes staring down "on all the tragic scene" below them. Yeats's version presents heroic stoicism as a positive value, whereas Auden's work is antiheroic. And while Yeats disdains to make a populist appeal, Auden in the *Musée* does make one—but only, it turns out, to assert the ultimate authority of the Old Masters, the authority of the aesthetic sanctum where the understanding of what is "human" is preserved. The "human" is a little idol appropriated to serve the *Musée* and its ministers, the Old Masters.

2

Up to this point we've treated the work as a self-referring machine. We've bracketed off the referent, which is not only the world the work refers to, but the world in which we and it are situated. In bracketing off that world, pretending it does not exist, we have been observing the decorum posed by the *Musée*. Which means that while we have considered rough structural elements of the *Musée*, we have done so uncritically; there has been no real attempt to step outside the terms imposed by the work. Yet what the *Musée* brackets off, or banishes from its authoritative precincts, is its own meaning. In suppressing its referent the *Musée* cloaks itself in the terms of a 16th-century rural, one might say Arcadian, setting. It trades on a painting that in *its* context, as a social practice in *its* time, debunked the classic mythology which was then being revived—a painting that, again in its time, opened up whatever passed for The Museum, making it not only accommodate but feature ordinary contemporary life *in the terms of* that life. Brueghel's ship is a contemporary ship, his plough a contemporary plough. But what is presented in the poem, as distinguished from the painting, is a carefully delimited costume drama.

In Auden's *Musée* there is neither the paraphernalia nor the technology of contemporary life. In this, too, Auden has something in common with Yeats, who played tennis and rode in autos, but who for tactical, ultimately political, reasons could not admit them into the 'world' of his poetry. Ordinarily Auden could accommodate the contemporary. But to admit these *here* would call attention to the suppression compelling the *Musée* to exist in the first place. The offhanded maneuvering, and the determination to deny historical specificity, suggest that this is neither critical commentary on a painting nor the working out of an antiquarian impulse. As we know, the suppressed behaves like the psychologically repressed: it oozes back into the site, the poem. So the miraculous birth introduces martyrdom and torture. We may wonder what lurks outside the walls, the lines, of this bucolic *Musée*. The allusions to martyrdom and torture, though muted, are more provocative than need be, given the structural project of the poem: a project simply to carry out crisis management by confining crises, and potential moral dilemmas, within a belittling perspective. The crises need not have been so serious.

3

Dyads are not neutral. However balanced they seem in abstraction, one of the terms must be *historically* privileged over the other. Any dyad bespeaks a subject-position; it testifies to the assumptions and values that define the site wherein it has been constructed. When 'white' and 'black' are applied to people, even if the terms are used 'impartially,' their mere existence defines a site where race is (as it need not be) a category, a significance, and a value. And when, in the *Musée*, the art of the Masters is art coached by quotidian life (art and life forming one dyad) and when that art and that life, in their mutual calm, are set over against miraculous, suffering or catastrophic life, life in extremis (another dyad), and when the changeless, 'natural' terms of the *Musée* are purged of disruptive terms from the historical world, the world we live in—all this defines a site where aesthetics overrides ethics, and normative terms are replaced by descriptive ones which in turn are taken as normative. It is a site where 'being' is a category, and 'becoming' is not—where oppositions are static, and nothing may happen. A site where quietism is a value.

For all the show of insouciance—the *just*, the *specially*, the *anyhow*, the *for instance*, the *quite*, the nearly colloquial *dreadful*—the *Musée* is not a museum of objective disinterest. It is an orientation. We are herded into a strictly defined site of meaning and value. The subject-position of the *Musée* has apparently been framed by the Old Masters, who (like Auden) see but are not seen. But the Old Masters, whoever they may be, have framed nothing. Brueghel notwithstanding, they remain anonymous and invisible functionaries. Having no identity, and therefore no opportunity for expression or initiative, they must be what Auden/*Musée* makes of them. The strategy of the poem demands it. The *Musée* invests the Old Masters with all authority, including the tone of authority. To have named them, or to have said outright that the Old Masters understood the human position of suffering and *never* made a mistake about it, might have invited demurral. But to intone almost with resignation, as if passing on a truism, that

> About suffering they were never wrong...

is something else again. Who were never wrong? Oh, the Old Masters. The point is not whether they understood—a disallowed question—but how *well* they did. The *Musée* is a kind of box. Its terms define the available space, and then proceed to fill it in. What they fill it with is us.

We need not, in a fit of anti-intellectualism, abandon hope and submit to the subject-position that has been constructed for us. We may introduce critical difference into this site, this *Musée*. But to do that we have to ask what specifically is *not* the subject-position. It is not that of suffering, nor of martyrdom, nor of the aged who hope for a future, an intervention, for something to happen (which is what the "miraculous birth" signifies, as opposed to the changeless present of the Old Masters "[who] were never wrong"). The subject-position is not that of the tortured, who do not exist even as a noun. And it is not that of Icarus, who is no longer Icarus but white legs disappearing into green water.

If the subject-position of the Old Masters is not that of suffering, what is the "human position of suffering" that they understand so well? The human position of suffering—the position of suffering they know to be humanly appropriate—is that it is remote. Even when near it is remote, distanced by sensory immediacy and self-absorption, which is the self-absorption of those who are not suffering. It is the suffering of *the other*. Not that the *Musée*'s Old Masters understand that suffering—they don't—but they do understand that it is human to be preoccupied with the immediate and the mundane. What is not the human position, in the view of the *Musée*, is concern for the suffering. Here any concern would be inordinate—would be, doubtless, another version of the "hysterical women" in Yeats's "Lapis Lazuli," that contemporaneous *Musée* of a slightly different cast.

Of course, there is no "human position" on suffering or anything else. There are positions, some flatly contradictory of the one projected here. But why does Auden define and organize "human" reality in this way? Rather, why *did* he? Why settle on this particular painter, or that painting by this painter? There are other Brueghel paintings, such as the *Massacre of the Innocents*, which tell a different story. There are painters, comparably old and 'masterly,' who assumed quite another subject-position. Why wasn't this poem, as distinct from that painting, writ from the subject-position of the suffering? Or of the empathetic? But then why even introduce suffering, martyrdom and torture into the poem? They aren't 'in' the painting. Icarus is a spectacular disaster, but historically as a rule the disaster has been rendered more as a moral, a meaning, than as an experience. (Perhaps because flight itself has not, until recently, been available as an experience.) The fall of Icarus has not ordinarily been associated with suffering, and it certainly isn't given that emphasis in Brueghel's comic treatment. So why key the poem to that? One thing is clear: whatever Auden's reasons for going beyond spectacle, he went beyond what, on the internal evidence, he *had* to contend with. But why?

One of Auden's weaknesses, also a strength, is that he cannot settle easily into aestheticism—a legacy perhaps of his formative period, as regards both literary influences (Brecht) and extra-literary ones (the Depression, the Spanish Civil War). Not that he doesn't aestheticize. On the contrary: a major project of the *Musée* is the distancing of suffering and the aestheticizing of that distancing. Still Auden cannot, as less conscious and less interesting poets do, aestheticize by exclusion. He does not cultivate ignorance. He tries immunization, defusing the extra-aesthetic by absorbing and transforming it. But there's a risk in this. The irritant to be pearled over, even if it's as backgrounded and anachronized as the allusion to torture (there being no tortured but also no torturer, and no modern torture equipment, only the rump of a horse giving torture an idyllic aura), may indecorously reassert itself and demand to be faced up to. Auden's tactical problem is a bit like that of John Berryman's "Henry" in one of his *Dream Songs*—it is the risk of cutting the body up and hiding the pieces "where they may be found." The act of suppression itself calls attention to the suppressed.

4

At this point we have to do something we're not supposed to do. We have to resurrect the historical context of the *Musée*, that being as much the text as the words on the page are. This will not prove anything, but it may highlight details and connections that are not, in a dehistoricized or historically unconscious mode, noticeable.

Auden was never actually a Marxist. Nor is there evidence that he had effective class-consciousness. But he had been 'socially committed,' had in a personalized way made poetic gestures on behalf of workers, and had dedicated some of his work and himself to the "war against fascism" in general and to the Spanish Civil War (1936-39) in particular. By the time of the *Musée* he was dropping all that and emigrating to the U.S., which he did on January 18, 1939. His reasons were not entirely political. There was the matter of his sexual life, and money. Nonetheless it was obvious that war was about to break out, and Auden had written himself into a public bind. That bind, which his writing had sealed, had less to do with sex or money than with politics. He had so committed himself in print, having 'stood up to be counted' in the fight against fascism, that his political disengagement occasioned awkwardness, some of which would be internalized. He was concerned lest his grand rhetorical gestures seem, in retrospect, to have been merely rhetorical. To ease his about-face seems to have been the effective *and* conscious project of the *Musée*, though the subtextual anxiety haunting this labor is tremendous. Consider, if you will, that Icarus was trying to escape the labyrinth of Daedalus's self-imprisoning art. Icarus did not succeed, but in the *Musée* Auden presents that failure (to escape the confines of art) as a success. Not for Icarus, certainly, who is little more than a disappearing, featureless whiteness, but for us—we who have been settled back into the Old Masterly subject-position constructed for us by the *Musée*. The poem, then, is most intent on rationalizing a move *back into art*.

In 1933 Auden had written to "comrades" in the factories:

> On you our interests are set
> Your sorrow we shall not forget
> While we consider
> Those who in every country town
> For centuries have done you brown,
> But you shall see them tumble down
> Both horse and rider.

In the name of those comrades he had attacked mystics, whose "cream of Heaven is the same / As any bounder's," the intellectuals' pose of dispassionate balance, and liberals "smarmy with friendship." Auden's targets may have been politically defined, but his terms were not. He could not get beyond 'prepolitical' snappishness and adrenal disgust. Nonetheless he did assume a principled position and had even upbraided the escapist, sensuously self-regarding poet:

> Unhappy poet, you whose only
> Real emotion is feeling lonely
> When suns are setting;
> Who fled in horror from all these
> To islands in your private seas
> Where thoughts like castaways find ease
> In endless petting:
>
> You need us more than you suppose
> And you could help us if you chose...

These auguring lines from "A Communist to Others" were later suppressed by the poet himself. In time Auden would rationalize quietism, making something remarkably similar to the "unhappy poet" the measure of the human. But the rationalization did not come easily. In different poems of the time he took just about every position imaginable, by turns defending, ridiculing and squirming over his abandonment of political struggle. A number of former political allies vilified him for having sold out. Meanwhile he wrote obsessively about writers and intellectuals, past and present. Through them he could conduct his own self-serving yet troubled argument. Referring to Julien Benda's *La Trahison des clercs* (1927), the notorious attack on intellectuals who serve political ends rather than devote themselves to 'universal spiritual values,' Auden petitions Henry James to "pray for me and for all writers living or dead," and to "make intercession / For the treason of all clerks" ("At the Grave of Henry James"). And in "Voltaire at Ferney," published in March 1939, after acknowledging the enemies that Voltaire in exile had left behind, Auden both defends and questions Voltaire's position before concluding that his former political project (Voltaire's, and by correspondence Auden's own) had been sustained by moral compromise:

> Far off in Paris, where his enemies
> Whispered that he was wicked, in an upright chair
> A blind old woman longed for death and letters. He would write
> 'Nothing is better than life'. But was it? Yes, the fight
> Against the false and the unfair
> Was always worth it. So was gardening. Civilize.
>
> Cajoling, scolding, scheming, cleverest of them all,
> He'd led the other children in a holy war
> Against the infamous grown-ups, and, like a child, been sly
> And humble when there was occasion for
> The two-faced answer or the plain protective lie,
> But, patient like a peasant, waited for their fall.

After equating the value of "the fight / Against the false and the unfair" with the value of "gardening," he slips into a position nearer that of the *Musée*. Voltaire's sense of moral responsibility is made to seem presumptuous, and so immoderate as to be pathological and futile.

> So, like a sentinel, he could not sleep. The night was full of wrong,
> Earthquakes and executions. Soon he would be dead,
> And still all over Europe stood the horrible nurses
> Itching to boil their children. Only his verses
> Perhaps could stop them: He must go on working. Overhead
> The uncomplaining stars composed their lucid song.

Voltaire is belittled, but so too the impending catastrophe in Europe: the childlike nightmare of boogie(wo)men, the "horrible nurses / Itching to boil their children." In place of the Old Masters in the *Musée* there are the "uncomplaining stars" who (yes, who) are also artists, and also above it all.

5

Auden was becoming the poet of uselessness, of helplessness, of turning away and sailing calmly on. By implication he saw himself as one of the surviving pieces of the broken "Godhead," a bit like a refugee from the metaphysical breakdown and disarray to which Arnold's "Dover Beach" testifies—someone for whom, in the telltale conclusion to "Herman Melville," there remained only to sit down at his desk and write a story. When, in "In Memory of W. B. Yeats," he writes that "poetry makes nothing happen"—that poetry, tucked away "in the valley of its saying," is nothing executives would want to tamper with—Auden is not *at that point* complaining. Immediately, superficially, he's discounting Yeats's grandiosity. But also (a circumstance less evident in the later, self-censored version of the poem) he is writing off Yeats's volkish, fascist-corresponding politics. In the three stanzas later suppressed, Auden had offered a belletrist apologia for Kipling, the voice of classic British imperialism, and Paul Claudel, the French Catholic reactionary who was to become a 'passive' supporter of the Vichy government's collaboration with the Nazi occupation of France. (Claudel's name would continue to be fraught with significance. During the May 1968 student/worker revolt in France, "No More Claudels!" was one of the slogans that appeared on the walls of the Sorbonne.) What is curious, perhaps in retrospect a giveaway, is that Auden's arbitrary *stand* is set forth in such assertive, unqualified terms.

> Time that is intolerant
> Of the brave and innocent,
> And indifferent in a week
> To a beautiful physique,
>
> Worships language and forgives
> Everyone by whom it lives;
> Pardons cowardice, conceit,
> Lays its honors at their feet.
>
> Time that with this strange excuse
> Pardoned Kipling and his views,
> And will pardon Paul Claudel,
> Pardons him for writing well.

Strange excuse indeed. But then Auden is not simply displaying the magnanimity of a leftist writer extending a guildish hand to a few discredited rightists who also happen to be writers. He is not transcending his own history and politics so as to go on record with special pleading on behalf of Kipling, Claudel and Yeats. He needed an excuse for his own "cowardice" or "conceit" or whatever it was that made him abandon, in effect turn on, the cause he had championed. (The Old Masters also need an excuse. Their remoteness would be suspect were it not underwritten by the indifference of ordinary people—the source of '30s leftish moral and political authority—living ordinary lives. That is, the Old Masters' understanding is sanctioned by the leftist populism that, like rightist folkism, follows from the Romantic ideal of an "organic society.") In writing off their fascism, dissolving political substance regardless of political character, Auden divested himself of his own political commitment without having to be up front about it. He was granting *himself* a pardon.

When Auden says there is nothing to be done, it means he need not choose to do nothing. He may cultivate a fateful air, and the nothing will be done *for* him. He absolves himself of responsibility, including responsibility to his own history, on the grounds of poetic indisposition. "Poetry makes nothing happen." It just goes on, or along. Not that such poetry is therefore useless—it isn't. It's useful not only *while* it is socially ineffectual, but *because* it is. With the seemingly privileged space and social disinterest of poetry, its freedom from the taint of practicality, of ulterior motives and hidden agendas, the displacement of speech with social silence becomes more credible. The 'observation' that poetry makes nothing happen, like the observation that it's human to overlook suffering, torture and martyrdom, is not an observation but a position. The poetry that makes nothing happen *makes* nothing happen.

6

Icarus falling, and the ship sailing on, are images of flight and destination. But one fails, one goes on. The crisis flight comes to disaster, the jaunty business-as-usual leaves all that behind. 'Turning away' and 'getting away' become the human thing to do. The poem masks this equation, however, presenting the 'getting away' as a 'getting on' with it (life). What had seemed to be the horns of a dilemma—the demands of ordinary life versus the passing attraction of the critical or the spectacular—turns out to be no dilemma at all. The problematic has been dissolved.

We might reconsider the subject-position of the poem by looking at the title: "*Musée des Beaux Arts*". Through it we are ushered into the understanding of the Old Masters, and through that understanding we are led down to the rhythmically and 'adjectively' aestheticized ship. This is not the only point in Auden's work where ships are exemplary aesthetic objects. The post-World War II "Fleet Visit" starts off with sailors on leave who "neither make nor sell—/ No wonder they get drunk." But, it concludes,

> ...their ships on the vehement blue
> Of this harbour actually gain
> From having nothing to do;
> Without a human will
> To tell them whom to kill
> Their structures are humane
>
> And, far from looking lost,
> Look as if they were meant
> To be pure abstract design
> By some master of pattern and line,
> Certainly worth every cent
> Of the billions they must have cost.

Here, too, the confirmation of humanity, its measure, is the aestheticized object. Its virtues are those of the painting coming into vogue during that postwar time: it was abstracted, and it had "nothing to do." The *Musée* is about choosing that object, which is also an 'objectivity.' It is about *coming to terms* with socially and ethically disarmed aesthetic values.

There's a '30s complement and contrast to Auden's ships-as-aesthetic-objects. It is William Carlos Williams's 1935 poem "The Yachts," which as Paul Mariani notes was occasioned by Williams's recollection of "the...America's Cup yacht races he had seen off Newport, Rhode Island, and the ambivalence he had felt watching all that aristocratic skill while knowing that it was a nation of poor people who in reality supported this small privileged class." Williams's poem helps us reconsider Auden's vessels because it resituates the yachts in the midst of their human cost. Williams presents the yachts as youthful, rare, feckless. They are tended to, groomed, like fine racehorses. Nonetheless Williams, unlike Auden, envisions them less in terms of aesthetic effect than of social cost. He *experiences* them from the position of all who have no share in their elegance and freedom—those who comprise the very waves bearing (up under) the yachts. The anthropomorphized waves "strike at" the yachts which are, however, "too / well made, they slip through, though they take in canvas." The conclusion is almost less apocalyptic— though it is that—than indignantly orgiastic:

Arms with hands grasping seek to clutch at the prows.
Bodies thrown recklessly in the way are cut aside.
It is a sea of faces about them in agony, in despair

until the horror of the race dawns staggering in the mind
the whole sea become an entanglement of watery bodies
lost to the world bearing what they cannot hold. Broken,

beaten, desolate, reaching from the dead to be taken up
they cry out, failing, failing! their cries rising
in waves still as the skillful yachts pass over.

Contemporary reviewers did not hesitate to read Williams's poem as political commentary. In contrast, Auden's is read largely as freefloating timeless 'poetry'— perhaps because the *Musée*'s subject-position is not that of

"The Yachts" but of the yachts themselves. The *Musée* as Old Slicksides.

7

Auden's poem condenses, incorporates, a decision. This is not obvious however. The structure puts us in the position not only of not choosing but of not having to choose, as though there were no decision to be made anyway. We are funneled into the perspective of everyday, self-absorbed, ignorant (ignoring) life. At the same time we must be persuaded to accept, as though it were our very ordinary own, the position we have been structured into. Auden wastes no time in trotting out the village elders, the Old Masters. Through them the poem imposes another distinction—not between the ordinary and the extraordinary but between the intensities of life, including moral intensities, and an imperturbable art. Having been ushered into the presence of the Old Masters, who know what they know, we are brought to a conclusion with the expensive delicate ship—a vehicle that, unlike the wings of Icarus, promises safe conduct. Yet this conclusion too rests on a false bottom. It is less a conclusion than a dissolution, or short-circuiting, of the social/aesthetic problematic.

The *Musée* is performative. It confers humanly superior status on the refusal of grand, social, 'other' concern. And it naturalizes that refusal. What had seemed an appeal to the perspective of ordinary life turns out to be an argument for the transcendent perspective, the ultimate *human* value, of art. 'Ordinary life' sanctions qualm-free self-absorption, which is hypostatized in the art of the Old Masters. What's puzzling, at first, is that although 'ordinary life' is the court and standard appealed to, there is little respect for ordinary life as such, which is presented in a perfunctory, at times deprecatory, manner. Like most demagogic appeals this bears little affection for the demos.

That's not the only crack in the *Musée*. Auden can't obliterate the contemporary historical context, which sifts through on the rumor of suffering and torture, but he may consign it to 'period piece' background detail. Even if he were capable of suppressing that context entirely, he couldn't— because the present *must be* present if he is to immunize himself against it. The *Musée* must be understood, or felt, to relate to the world *now*. The understanding of the Old Masters must appear timeless yet apposite to the present. Even desituated period pieces—what Osip Mandelstam disdainfully referred to as paper lanterns—must, to realize their 'universal' meaning, be historically appropriated.

8

The *Musée* is supported, even as it is undermined, by logical impasses. As has been noted, the ordinary is privileged over the extraordinary. Yet the privileged 'ordinary' is also ordinary in a negative sense. It hovers at the level of bodily functions, of scratching or eating. In the structuration of the poem, and the values generated through it, doggy life is life on the plane of the skating children. On a par, willy-nilly, with the horse's behind and the ploughman. The only prized or enhanced life, that of the ship, transcends the ordinary by virtue of being "expensive" and "delicate." The ship goes about its business just as the dogs go on with their doggy life. In this there is equivalence. There is no equivalence, however, in their respective significances.

The opposition between ordinary and extraordinary, an opposition *at first* privileging the former, should lead to a subject-position sited with the ordinary. Structural and narrative logic demand that we identify with the ploughman, seeing and valuing as he supposedly sees and values. But the *Musée* presumes to transcend itself, to stand outside the structuration of its own values. It justifies the privileging of ignorance over knowledge, of indifference over concern, only to claim that the ignorance and indifference constitute a metahistorical knowledge—that of the Old Masters who were never wrong. Those who live that knowledge, doing what comes 'naturally' in a time-warp where nothing happens, nonetheless live in ignorance of it. Knowledge proper is reserved for their superiors, the Old Masters, in *their* timeless warp.

At this we might pause. We could go on accepting the terms of the *Musée*, though holding it accountable for them— or we could break the spell, go outside the structure and historicize it. We could return to questions raised earlier: which Old Masters? Those of Pisa or Orvieto? Bosch, Dürer, Goya? Or so much other work by Brueghel? These and other Old Masters had quite another view of suffering and its "human position." By citing them we could become critical subjects of the *Musée*. We could refuse to be its objects, mere functions of its imposing ground rules. We could put this museum's Old Masters up against the wall of history, including art history. We could say, you can't substitute poetic truth for historical truth. Certainly, not all the Old Masters understood what Auden says they did. Even if this were an accurate reading (as though there could be, as there cannot be, one monolithic reading of a monolithic category called "Old Masters"), or if this were what a few Old Masters knew about the "human position" of suffering—*was that a knowledge or an ideology*? Was it a truth about nature, human nature, or a social project on behalf of a predetermined interest? By posing such questions we might expose the *Musée*'s "Old Masters" as being not historical figures, not data, but a metaphysical first principle, a concoction. If those Old Masters did not exist—and as summarized and reduced in the *Musée* they did not—they would have to be invented. And they were.

9

The *Musée* constructs its own high ground: a superior vantage point from which it may perceive that indifference and ignorance are quintessentially human. Yet more significant than the 'perception' is the assumption that there is a human nature. In nature the human is indistinguishable from the animal: human life comes to the same thing as "doggy life"; the human is as irreducibly natural as the torturer's horse's behind is. The ultimate transcendental subject, then, is not the human, but nature itself. Nature—human or animal, it makes no difference—may be noted but not questioned. There is nothing to be done about it. And that is the point. The human, interpreted as the 'naturally' human, is treated as a given rather than as a problematic (as an answer rather than as a complex of historically conditioned questions).

Nonetheless, the concluding and conclusive critical distinction is not between human and animal, who merge in 'nature,' but between art and life, aesthetics and ethics. If truth is humdrum, beauty need not be. Though the art of the Old Masters is an art of understanding, it need not be doggy, like the life it takes its understanding from. That, in part, is why the ultimate art image, the ship—also a vehicle for unconcern and incomprehension—is presented as almost studiously, provocatively precious. Its ornamental indifference has an air of superior breeding. For a moment, as it moves with the anapestic languor of the lady in Pound's "The Garden," the unconcern of the expensive delicate ship crystallizes the project of the poem. Even as it apprehends a 'truth,' a 'reality,' the ship projects itself beyond that. The undeterred ship has "somewhere to get to," and sails calmly on. Its errand is not its own, however, but Master Auden's.

10

So much for "the human position of suffering." What began as a demagogic appeal to people (meaning ordinary people) in terms of what they do (meaning what they ordinarily do) gives the last word, actually a dehistoricized image, to the "expensive delicate" subject-position leaving the scene of the disaster. But the "human" has already been defined as uncaring. According to the *Musée*, to turn away is the "human" thing to do. Art is making this natural: casting suffering and catastrophe in Arcadian tones. Had this work occupied the subject-position of the suffering, or had the suffering been obviously political, we might have called it propaganda. But as it does not, we need not. We may take the *Musée* for what it is: a real belles-lettres poem, a work that masters history and logic, including its own.

THE DREAM OF AN APOLITICAL POETRY

I should call a wolf to shine the mirror of the sheep
That forgot their own image...
—Adonis (Ali Ahmad Sa'id),
"The Desert: The Diary
of Beirut under Siege, 1982"

1 Gauguin away, Woolf at home

THE DREAM OF AN APOLITICAL POETRY IS THE DREAM OF GETTING
AWAY FROM ALL THIS. THE DREAM, IN A HOUSE NOT ONE'S OWN, OF A
ROOM OF ONE'S OWN.

We need not, like Gauguin fleeing the brokerages of Europe
for a Pacific 'nature' administered as the French colonies of
Tahiti and the Marquesas, torment ourselves with cosmic
questioning on behalf of an undifferentiated humanity. We
cannot ask what we are, as Gauguin's famous triptych does
on its bed of sackcloth, without asking who, when, where, or
how gendered, raced, nationed, in what mixes, how weighted
or handicapped, and within what class. (In life, if not in
painting, neither could Gauguin, who was accused of
instigating the Polynesians to revolt "because I tell them what
are their rights.")[1] Nor can we presume that art may be
insulated from business, or livelihood dissociated from art.
We are implicated, situated, and we bear that fact. Literatures
are no less conditioned, situated, inscribed. They too have no
elsewhere to flee to, no island in the Pacific, no beyond.

[Gauguin, already in Tahiti: "I said to myself the time had
come to clear out and go to a simpler country with fewer
officials. And I thought of packing my trunks and moving to
the Marquesas. They promised land, more land than they
knew what to do with, meat, fowl, and, to guide you there, a

47

gendarme as gentle as a lamb…Straightaway, with my heart
at ease, as trusting as an unobstructed virgin, I took the boat
and arrived calmly in Atuona…"]

WHERE DO WE COME FROM, WHAT ARE WE

When Virginia Woolf was asked to speak on women and
fiction, she hardly knew where to begin. So she began at
home, with the *institutional* homes of "Oxbridge" university
and library with their prohibitions against her. Prohibitions
against straying from the gravel path. Against entering the
library without an escort or, at least, a letter of introduction.
But then her investigations could not begin there, either, for
in considering how women in general live, she could only ask
how women *have* lived, "not throughout the ages, but in
England, say in the time of Elizabeth." Woolf, having chosen
her target, was holding the mirror up to our assumptions
about literature, especially the 'transcendent' literature of
Shakespeare. Why, she asked, was there no female
Shakespeare?

> For it is a perennial puzzle why no woman wrote a word of
> that extraordinary literature when every other man, it
> seemed, was capable of song or sonnet. What were the
> conditions in which women lived, I asked myself:
> for…imaginative work…is like a spider's web, attached ever
> so lightly perhaps, but still attached to life at all four corners.
> Often the attachment is scarcely perceptible; Shakespeare's
> plays…seem to hang there complete by themselves. But
> when the web is pulled askew, hooked up at the edge, torn
> in the middle, one remembers that these webs are not spun
> in midair by incorporeal creatures, but are the work of
> suffering human beings, and are attached to grossly material
> things, like health and money and the houses we live in.[2]

There could be no female Shakespeare because "in real life [the Elizabethan woman] could hardly read, could scarcely spell, and was the property of her husband." If 'genius' cannot read, spell or speak for itself, then it can hardly be articulated as literature.

It is utterly coincidental that when Gauguin attempted to answer his own question, "where are we going," he could only come up with the portentous image of "an old woman near to death." Yet it is not so curious that while pressing in different directions Woolf and Gauguin would speak similar desires: a room of one's one, or a hut of one's own, in a world not one's own. An island in a world where there is none, a privileged space where one's privilege construes another's deprivation. As if that knot were not difficult enough to undo, they were caught up also in their own contradictions (as who would not be). One was marginalized by gender, privileged by class. The other, a de facto colonialist dying alone, in agony, poverty-stricken in a hut stocked with wines and tins of luxury foods, and shunned by the European colony as "a heretic." But finally Gauguin and Woolf were beating their heads against different walls of the same massive, global establishment—which later, redesigned to preserve and extend itself, would mortise them also into its walls.

[Gauguin filed complaints: about "gendarmes spying on the village girls bathing, then arresting them for indecency; a girl appealing for protection against rape being raped in turn by the magistrate who dismissed the case." Such stories *were* the story. The vaguely symbolic metaphysic with which he vested his painting merely obscured the nightmarish reality that he could engage and write about, but could not paint. The painting remained symptomatic, a reaction *within* the colonial configuration: that routine wherein the judge rapes the one who petitions for justice. Gauguin too was subjected to the ritual of colonial justice. When he submitted to the authorities a detailed list of injustices done to the native population, his petition was declared libelous, proceedings were instituted against him, and he was condemned to three months imprisonment and a fine of 1,000 francs.]

2   Bermudas

THE DREAM OF APOLITICAL POETRY IS THE DREAM OF WRITING ON A BLANK SHEET OF PAPER.

The poetry of Shakespeare's sister, if there was a sister, does not exist. It was not allowed to. But what of the literature that does? The Anglo-American canon of non-peasant, non-laborer, white males—a northern hemispheric canon which, significantly, excludes the English-speaking Caribbean. Wasn't this the literature that would follow in the wake of Andrew Marvell's mind, transcending even "its own resemblance": an imaginative literature outstripping sources and occasions to arrive at "far other worlds, and other seas…"? A literature

> Annihilating all that's made
> To a green thought in a green shade…
> —"The Garden"[3]

Isn't that what literature does? Isn't this the freedom of the poetic imagination: to be the end of thought, rather than its beginning? Doesn't poetry, true poetry, ascend the tower with Yeats, say, to dream and so create "Translunar Paradise"?

Often enough it seems to. Many poetries create 'worlds' by blotting out the one they exist in. Their triumph is to conceive lands without people.

[Gauguin recounts a fiction that "officials, who always know so much," repeat to visitors who come ashore at Tahiti: namely, that all Maoris come from the Malay Archipelago, hence there are no natives of Oceania. That is, no Polynesians *as such.* The French colonial administration wanted to make the French colonists as 'native' as the Polynesians, thus with as much 'right' to Oceania. Gauguin observes, acidly, that this fable has been "adopted and regurgitated by all the photographers." Officials and photographers (in Gauguin's eyes, identical) are astonished at "the very idea of the ancient land of Oceania churning out men!" He concludes in exasperation: "In what era did men begin to exist on this globe of ours...?" *Three different human groups had been migrating to Oceania as far back as the Pleistocene epoch, over 11,000 years ago—surely enough time to achieve status as 'natives.'*]

But native populations and historical givens, on-the-ground facts, are an embarrassment not only to colonists but to 'apolitical' poetries as well. Neither colonists nor poets stake out vacant lots. Marvell's "Bermudas" is unusual in that it celebrates an actual world where the native population did not have to be suppressed, appropriated or driven out. "For the islands of the Barmudas, as every man knoweth that hath heard or read of them, were never inhabited by any Christian or heathen people..." (Sylvester Jourdain, 1610). There was no native population, or if there was, it has been expunged from the Spanish and English historical record. That population is, then, a kind of Shakespeare's sister: struck dumb, so that even if it should have happened to exist, it does not.

IN THE PROTOCOL OF THE ANGLO-AMERICAN CANON, MARVELL'S "BERMUDAS" IS BERMUDAN LITERATURE.

"Bermudas" may be based on accounts of Sir George Somers's shipwreck, in 1609, involving English colonists on their way to Virginia (a narrative also contributing to Shakespeare's *Tempest*), but the poem was certainly informed by the Bermudan experiences of John Oxenbridge, the 'Oxbridge' in whose household Marvell had worked. It begins with sailors or settlers in the "Oceans bosome unespy'd," singing:

> What should we do but sing his Praise
> That led us through the watry Maze,
> Unto an Isle so long unknown,
> And yet far kinder than our own?

Safe from storms "and prelate's rage," the solution to the riddle of the "watry Maze," this land turns out to be an eternal Spring inventory of oranges, pomegranates, figs, melons, apples, cedars of Lebanon, ambergris and natural religion. There is not a soul on it. That, in a way, is the beauty of it. This is God's Country, and it is exceedingly pleasant. Ordinarily, colonialist literatures must eradicate the 'other' by defining it as inferior or nonhuman (*The Tempest*'s Caliban, Robinson Crusoe's cannibals, his loving Xury and devoted man[servant] Friday, the brutes deep in the *Heart of Darkness*, humanoid apes in *Tarzan of the Apes*—or gendered as the reptilian queen, preferably Asiatic, in comic book adventure stories), by appropriating it under the cover of 'civilizing' it, or by measuring it against standards of 'civilization.' But in "Bermudas" that is not necessary. The rowers' song is a song of empire triumphant. Especially triumphant because uncontested, without onus.

> Thus sung they, in the *English* boat,
> An holy and a chearful Note,
> And all the way, to guide their Chime,
> With falling Oars they kept the time.

Marvell's "Bermudas" may be one of the stillest poems on record: its motions are without movement, perfectly so, like clockhands rounding on themselves, going nowhere because they are always already there, anchored to that center which is the site of power, the so-called civilization tuning their movement. That motion without movement is, for sure, the politic of this 'apolitical' poetry in its *English* boat.

"THE CIVILIZED HORDES ARRIVE
AND RUN UP A FLAG"

[The Marquesas, 1902 or 03: "The Governor from Tahiti arrived in his yacht escorted by a French warship. Gauguin watched him leaning over the side of the yacht taking photographs of the romantically situated village, watched the foreign colony giving him a festive welcome, watched the Marquesan girls...showering flowers before him as he landed. He heard of festivities in the village—the processions, the banquets; heard too that the islanders had not been allowed to present him with a petition of their grievances—and watched the Governor sail away as ignorant of the truth as when he arrived." He sent a sarcastic memorandum after the Governor at Papeete: "When you look at those superb photographs you have taken, it will be evident to you that this is a delightful country where beauty, *joie de vivre* and a luxuriant vegetation conspire to make everyone happy."]

[Gauguin, 12 January 1900: "The civilized hordes arrive and run up a flag; the fertile ground becomes arid, the rivers dry up; no more perpetual holiday—instead, a struggle for survival, and constant labor...The storm passes by over our heads, bowing the tops of the age-old coconut trees down to the ground...They poison our land with their infected excrement...they sterilize the soil, deface and damage living matter...Everything perishes..."]

3   stone imagination

THE DREAM OF POLITICAL POETRY IS NO DREAM.

In 1948 the Polish writer Tadeusz Różewicz published "Stone Imagination," a key formulation in his project to reconstitute a physical *and mental* world from that laid waste in the World War II invasion and occupation of Poland.[4] Różewicz, a young man at the time, had seen the dismantling of every human truth, value and category he had held to be self-evident. Concepts were "but words." Love and hate, man and beast, friend and foe were little more than synonymous "labels." He had lived to see the humanly incomprehensible: a man "who was both / vicious and virtuous."

"Stone Imagination" reconsiders the imagination as is, in place. We might, to comprehend this undertaking, ask what Gauguin would have done were his life stuck in place. Rather, what might he have done with the realization *not in life only, where he realized this full well, but in art* that there is nowhere, not the Marquesas nor Tahiti, beyond the devastating reach of European commerce? Rather than scramble to deny or escape implication, which would only further implicate, Różewicz resists by turning to the mundane dreams, relieved or troubled, of the woman lying beside him

> with her thick gold braid
> she dreams she has broken a pitcher
> or found the keys
> or torn her dress

His own imagination, like hers yet desperate, at the edge, also cannot transcend. This, remember, is Poland after World War II. He knows "only" the taste of cinnamon

> yet I dream of exotic lands
> where cinnamon trees grow
> where sandalwood trees grow
> and that's as far as my poor head goes

my poor head. From two films
and a few books
I construct a landscape without color

Without color because available films and photos are in black
and white. At the same time he is teased by the sensuous
(sensual) postwar "western" abundance that measures, in fact
constructs, his own deprivation:

(don't laugh foreigners
especially you beautiful ladies out of magazines
French and American)

He tries to escape, to dream

a palm or two palms
and a round little island
oh it's not easy to construct
a picture beautiful unusual
so I add a tiger
that looks like a cat

He cannot get beyond homeliness. When at last he manages
to dream two pineapples, they bring him horribly to earth.
They are the

pineapples I saw before the war
in Rosenberg's store

Rosenberg will never see
the islands of the Pacific
the Ukrainians caught up with him in the sewer
he died drowned in excrement
you can't imagine
Rosenberg's death in a small town
near Piotrków in Poland

Who can't imagine? The "beautiful foreign ladies with bare/
white breasts." And "you." You can't imagine. Their, your,
imagination is also limited; it does not extend to the reality

of Rosenberg. *Your* imagination cannot comprehend the reality even of Różewicz. Which is to say your imagination, glutted with goods, cannot conceive this desolation.

Różewicz is left with "a bare picture" of bare breasts, with what exotica his imagination has grasped: a whale, a pearl, a black, the viceroy of India, an elephant, an octopus, "a fig tree (or rather the fruit of the fig tree)," an ostrich and Hawaiian guitars.

So it is so it is and that's all.

I look around the room
on the table is a white pitcher
and suddenly I begin thinking
about the moon but I won't reveal
these thoughts to anyone
even though half a lifetime has passed
(in our country the average is fifty years)
and those lands islands seas
are like small moons
unreal dead.

Thus the dream of transcendence ("translunar paradise"). Gauguin's painted Marquesas and Marvell's Bermudas, those poetries dreaming their apolitical islands, are with their islands "small moons / unreal dead." (Though there *is* historical specification, a sign of life, in the suspicious glances cast back at him, at us the viewers, by so many of Gauguin's models.) Still these are the poetries, the far other worlds and other seas, whose sole predication is to annihilate "all that's made." To Marvell's people-weary imagination, a green unpeopled thought is or was an ecstatic experience: was to be almost literally beside oneself, out-of-body, thus to complete the most exacting gesture of depopulation. And Gauguin in his desolation can only romance a noble savagery of natural elegance and beautiful proportion; the rapist judge and the camera governor have been banished from his painting. In the stone imagination of Różewicz there is precious little greenery. There are, however, people, not necessarily beautiful ones. The point is, *not one is expendable.* As he puts it in another poem, "In the Midst of Life":

> I sat in the doorway of my house
> that old woman who
> is leading a goat by a rope
> is more necessary
> and more precious
> than the seven wonders of the world
> anyone who thinks and feels
> that she is not necessary
> is a mass murderer

The stone imagination comes to this: not "an old woman near to death," but recognition *and assertion* of the enduring necessity of that woman. Różewicz is no Marvell. He does not, as Marvell does, take the addition of Eve, old or young, to be the diminishment of Paradise. On the contrary, his resolution is to "lie quietly beside / a woman with a thick gold braid":

> I who know only one taste
> the exotic taste of cinnamon
> an average man with an imagination
> stunted stone and implacable.

His admission, neither holy nor cheerful, is nonetheless triumphant: the proclamation of an imagination that does not budge. So what if there is no apolitical poetry, no desituated imagination, no transcendent plenitude? These are, after all, only barren attempts to get beyond what richness there is: the "thick gold braid" dreaming its actual life.

[And Gauguin? Having shuttled between Oceania and France, his last time there having gotten syphilis, his broken ankle unhealed and his legs swollen with eczema, returning to Oceania where he is cut off from both colonial and native populations, he produces his last bit of exotica: a landscape of Breton village houses, all roof, and snow-laden nearly to the ground.]

4   wolf, sheep, accounting for dreams

POLITICAL POETRY IS THE DREAM OF THE UNIMAGINABLE: WHAT IS.

When, in his verse diary written during the siege of Beirut, the Lebanese poet Adonis made a caustic offer to have the wolf show the sheep what they are, he was addressing his fellow Arabs. The Israeli "wolf" had shown the Arab "sheep" how far their militant talk had outstripped their military capability. The sheep had lost the ability to see themselves as they are. For this they had paid dearly.

So-called apolitical poetries, too, may be mirrorless sheep of a sort, misperceiving themselves, their powers and their functions. They are bound to be sheep—figments of any overriding systemic imagination—insofar as they fail to admit to, or account for, their situation and their reality. In themselves such poetries constitute no basis for struggle or production, no ground from which to begin. With them there is only the dream that poetry is one thing, politics another. The dream that Tahiti is not Paris, nor Bermudas London. The dream of an island in the sea that one may escape to. The dream that poetries *are* islands. So the dream of reason, of thinking on blank sheets, is not the only one to end in nightmare. The dream blot of an apolitical poetry also produces monsters: Calibans and cannibals, brutes and human apes, depopulated paradises and lands, stripped of their history, teeming with two-legged beasts. Its beauty predicates monstrosity as surely as wealth presumes (*constructs* and presumes) impoverishment.

58

[In desperation Gauguin wrote from the Marquesas to a newspaper in Paris: "MONSTROUS THINGS ARE HAPPENING HERE." The paper informed him that this "would not interest our readers." Gauguin, of course, had meant the monstrosity of the colonial church, the gendarmerie and its administration. "The Magistrate arrives...in a hurry to dispose of the accumulation of arrears, knowing nothing about them...nothing of what the natives are like, nothing of the matters except what is contained in the file submitted to him by the gendarme. Seeing before him a tattooed face, he says to himself: 'Here is a cannibal brigand.'" "I am," Gauguin declared with pride, "a savage."]

Yet there is another poetry. The poetry and dream of the stone imagination: the broken pitcher, the lost keys, the torn dress, the pineapples in the store window, the poetry dream of Rosenberg fleeing the Ukrainians, caught in the sewer and dying in shit. It is the dream of a tiger that looks like a cat. The dream of the unimaginable: what is. Who or what could have imagined it? Not an 'apolitical' poetry, certainly, with its expendable people and dismissible realities, its pristine grounds, its imagination premised on blank sheets of paper. Only the stone imagination of 'political' poetry might do justice to the range and depth of the humanity which, deliberately or not, we act constantly to define. Which is to say, construct.

[Gauguin on cannibalism: "Civilized people! You are proud of not eating human flesh. On a raft you would eat it...On the other hand, every day you eat your neighbor's heart." In this he seems to echo Montaigne, who considered cannibalism, roasting and eating a man "after he is dead," to be benign in comparison with religious and legal torture, dismemberment and execution: "I think there is more barbarism in eating men alive than to feed upon them being dead; to mangle by tortures and torments a body full of lively sense…" Do we give too much credit to 'apolitical' poetry in calling it a pallid reflection of the barbarism that Montaigne compares, unfavorably, with cannibalism?]

LETTER TO THE CANNIBALS

Dear cannibals
don't scowl
at a person
who asks if a seat is free
in a train compartment

please understand
other people also have
two legs and a rear

Dear cannibals
just a second
don't trample on the weaker
don't gnash your teeth

please understand
there are lots of people and there will be
many more move back a bit
make room

Dear cannibals
don't buy up all
the candles shoelaces and noodles
Don't say with backs turned:
I me my mine
my stomach my hair
my corns my trousers
my wife my children
my opinion

Dear cannibals
let's not eat each other up Okay
because we're not going to be resurrected
Really
　　　—Różewicz

Political poetry is not a contradiction in terms but an instructive redundancy. It does not hold the mirror up to nature. It holds social reality up to the sheep, showing poetry its own face, its condition, its grounds and horizons. Showing, finally, that there is no poetry that is not political, and that 'apolitical' and 'political' both have a political project—but one dreams transcendence, denial, immobility, blank expanses, whereas the other admits and treasures its problematical, restive, historied situation.

Here again, analogy breaks down. Life is truly unimaginable. There are sheep, and sheep. Some, like those Adonis writes of, end up as victims in every way, victims even of themselves. Others reach an accommodation, the quiet trauma that passes for life and livelihood. 'Apolitical' poetries may go along with murderous purposes, while 'political' poetries are buried alive. No poetry, of whatever sort, is ever the last word.

"WE LOST BUT LOVE GAINED NOTHING"

The Palestinian poet Mahmoud Darwish had a more introspective way of articulating the dilemma that Adonis, himself wolf-like, had held the mirror up to. In a poem also brought on by the siege of Beirut ("We Lost but Love Gained Nothing"), he would ask:

> How many dreams have we lost in our sleep while we were working,
> looking for bread in the rocks.

Perhaps Darwish is lamenting those hopes whose time has passed. Or rephrasing the anguish of Gauguin's half-

question, "where are we going." Where, enchained in exile, is
there to go?

> How many birds have flown around our windows while we were
> playing with our chains in a postponed day.

Playing with our chains? Perhaps this is simply (simply!)
regretful. Regretful that songs came to us "but we were
asleep," or regretful over "how many kisses" may have
"knocked on our door while we were asleep." Yet a more
empowering, constructive implication is that the songs, the
kisses and the birds are there all along, and that the more
devastating exile has been the internal one: the shutting out.

> How many dreams have we lost in our sleep while we were working,
> looking for bread in the rocks.

The lost dreams are with the work and the bread, as the poetry
is with the politic. One is not found apart from the other.
The loss, then, is neither in the dreaming nor in the working
but in the poetry that sleeps through it all, missing their
connection.

5   postscript: from rooms without lights

The French poet Paul Valéry wrote, "It is the very one who
wants to write down his dream who is obliged to be extremely
wide awake."[6] Wide awake, yes, but what about the rest of it?
The point is not to "write down" the dream (we are not
archivists, simply) but to *write* it. What then does it mean, in
a world which is not a blank sheet of paper, to write the
dream?

Contending with the politics of language in African
literature, the Kenyan writer Ngũgĩ wa Thiong'o states his
theme:

It is taken from a poem by the Guyanese poet Martin Carter in which he sees ordinary men and women hungering and living in rooms without lights; all those men and women in South Africa, Namibia, Kenya, Zaire, Ivory Coast, El Salvador, Chile, Philippines, South Korea, Indonesia, Grenada, Fanon's 'Wretched of the Earth,' who have declared loud and clear that they do not sleep to dream, 'but dream to change the world.'[7]

Later he remarks on his own arrest and imprisonment, in December, 1977 by the Kenyan government. Six weeks after one of his co-scripted (community-authored) plays had been banned, he found himself "in cell 16 at Kamiti Maximum Security Prison as a political detainee answering to a mere number K6,77. Cell 16 would become for me what Virginia Woolf had called *A Room of One's Own* and which she claimed was absolutely necessary for a writer. Mine was provided free by the Kenyan government." And so, he continues, "confined within the walls of that room of my own, I thought a great deal about my work in the Literature Department..."

The significance, for us, is that Ngũgĩ does not propose to create something out of nothing. Under the wide, dazed features of 'what is,' he attends to the talkback, the language of struggle, emerging from the nothing that is in reality so many teeming, unlighted rooms. Which is to say, this is *our* wake-up call.

1   Quotations by and about Gauguin are from the following books: Paul Gauguin, *Letters* (Cleveland: World Publishing Company, 1949); *The Writings of a Savage: Paul Gauguin*, edited by Daniel Guerin (New York: Viking, 1978); Henri Perruchot, *Gauguin* (Cleveland: World Publishing Company, 1963); Lawrence and Elisabeth Hanson, *Noble Savage: The Life of Paul Gauguin* (New York: Random House, 1955).

2   Virginia Woolf, *A Room of One's Own* (New York: Harcourt Brace Jovanovich, 1929, 1975), 43-44.

3   Marvell quotations are from *The Poems & Letters of Andrew Marvell*, H. M. Margoliouth, ed. (London: Oxford University Press, 1952).

4   Quotations are from Tadeusz Różewicz, *The Survivor and other poems*, translated by Magnus J. Krynski and Robert A. Maguire (Princeton, N.J.: Princeton University Press, 1976).

5   Verses by Adonis and Mahmoud Darwish are from *Modern Poetry of the Arab World*, edited and translated by Abdullah al-Udhari (New York: Penguin, 1986), pp. 73 and 142.

6   Paul Valéry, *The Art of Poetry* (London: Routledge & Kegan Paul, 1958), translated by Denise Folliot. The quotation is from the essay "Concerning *Adonis*."

7   Ngũgĩ wa Thiong'o, *Decolonising the Mind: The Politics of Language in African Literature* (London: James Currey/Heinemann, 1986).

SCRATCHING SURFACES

the social practice of tendency poetry

clandestine poems

Roque Dalton was a Marxist-Leninist militant of the Salvadoran Communist Party and of the People's Revolutionary Army (ERP). His poems, especially in *Poemas Clandestinos* (preferred source of these newly translated collections), are discursive, politically explicit.[1] They are what poems are not supposed to be. Worse, they're encouraging: heartening rather than consoling. They raise gritty issues with brio and devastating humor. Their clandestinity is a function of their outspokenness (the public, or eminent, domain having been claimed by social silence). I'm not about to address the articulated issues, however, nor the translations themselves. I'm concerned with the aesthetic ruins scattered about the feet of these resurrected, transfigured, unbowed poems. They so unsettle our aesthetic presumption that we have to ask what, in our notions of poetry, we have refused to admit. What poetry have we buried under our own dust. And why? The answer, or a clue to it, may be found where most are found: just beneath the surface of what seems too obvious for words. In this regard what seems self-evident is the incompatibility of didacticism and/or ideas, historically specific ideas, with what is designated "poetry."

preaching, didacticism, etc.

For many contemporary poets the injunction against preaching makes good aesthetic sense. It is also a moral imperative. It must be wrong "to tell people what to think." To believe otherwise will lead you to violate art *and* humanity.

Will make you cold, hard: a hammerhead. That anyway is the conventional wisdom. It makes sense. But how much, and whose sense is it?

What for now I'll call preaching (didacticism? sloganeering? pamphleteering? poetically indecorous prosiness?) is a catchall for a range of social practices, written and spoken. When "preaching" is charged against texts that are direct and impassioned, explicitly engaged with politics or social justice, we might ask what then is recommended: indirection? not saying what we think? not addressing certain aspects of life?[2] But tempting as this might be, even such questions as these, with their transparent effort to pass as answers, only deepen the mystification. Their terms are like those of a formal debate: the options share an internal logic, a common discourse, which is sustained by a sea of exclusions and suppressions. The seeming alternatives are no more than variations within an effectively monolithic social set. Here, for instance, by momentarily putting the conflict in terms of "content"—saying or not saying "what we think," talking or not talking "about certain things"—we have raised a pressing issue, but with it we have papered over what is more problematically *at* issue. More troubling and crucial than the isolable issues of "content" or "reference," there is the indissociable matter of conduct.

The provocation may be less what preaching is about than what it does. Any so-called preaching, especially within the precincts of the "aesthetic," may be condemned for reasons having less to do with subjects of preaching, encapsulated themes or contents, than with preaching as social practice. And that may be the problem. Preaching is discourse constituted as unembarrassed social practice. It *confronts*, troubling the hegemony of social silence. Even status quo preaching is met with ambivalence—because it strains the status quo, and in addressing ideology (which is by definition unconscious, pervasive, a way of naturalizing and living the web of social relations, and doing so in the

66

self-serving terms of class interest), it mortifies ideology, laying it open to critical analysis. The distinction of preaching is in the degree to which it admits its own condition as social practice.

saying

As we ordinarily use the word, preaching patronizes. But the opprobrium cast on that also smears poetries that are discursive, explicit about the social values that inform them. It would be more appropriate to call this, not preaching, but saying. *Saying* is what this is about.

What is the moral or aesthetic flaw in *saying?* Who says? And why? Must poetry be only symptomatic, a social function rather than social practice? A nonsaying comparable to hack teaching whereby a "problem" is posed and an "answer" (momentarily, yet in that moment signaling *power over)* is withheld? What poetic universe does that imply? One where motifs, themes, genres and dehistoricized forms drift in a void, occasionally having their numbers painted in. They might as well, because nothing adds up in such a world. And that's the point: nothing is supposed to. What is produced is not knowledge or social practice (which are transformative: "if you want to know the taste of the pear, you must change the pear by eating it yourself") but commodity exchange. A kind of dark ages filling up with sensible dead matter. Yet this commodity exchange is of lives frozen in social silence:

> Here in the University
> while I listen to a speech by the President
> (in each doorway there are state police
> making their contribution to culture)
> pale with disgust I recall
> the sad peace of my native poverty,
> the gentle slowness of death in my village.

My father is waiting back there.
I came to study
the architecture of justice,
the anatomy of reason,
to look for answers
to the terrible abandonment, the thirst.

Oh night of false lights,
tinsel made out of darkness:
where should I flee
if not into my own soul,
soul that wanted to be a flag returning home
and that now they want to turn into a filthy rag
in this temple of thieves?

—Roque Dalton
"Remembrance and Questions"
(Richard Schaaf, trans.)

social silence

What does social silence signify? Withholding what we think
from what we say, we treat thoughts as objects, things. (If we
cannot think without language—a debatable assumption
anyway—we can and do think without speaking or writing.)
In so doing we commodify thought, making it a property.
Though what's behind the hoarding, the metaphorical greed,
is fear. Social silence is fear.

Jameson has said that "the profound vocation of the work
of art in a commodity society [is] *not* to be a commodity, *not*
to be consumed…" It might seem that by withholding, or
trying to withhold, we refuse commodification. But what is
withheld, and from whom? In truth this is not the powerful
leaden silence of a Bartleby squatting in the nerve center of

commodity exchange, up against the wall, defiant to the end. This silence signifies accommodation, not resistance. Silence is job, career, acceptance. Silence, this silence, is golden.

Consumption occurs through our eating our own thoughtful words: self-censorship.

Language generates a more reverberant, spellbinding, insidious silence than "silence itself" does. Social silence may be projected as speech, writing, data or news. Then words are used reflexively, as screens, walls, mirrors facing in on their own ideological garden, which is what they cultivate. They become like Milton's serpent, the silence *within* speech.[3] Social silence may be called law, poetry, torture or tolerance. Or it may be named beauty, harmony, civilization, history (how much unimaginable silence is there in these). Whatever, it is the silence pressuring all lives to be opaque, self-preoccupied, impersonal, interchangeable and, it follows, redundant. Lives become commodities that they may be, in the perverse logic of this system, valuable. Meanwhile, socially sanctioned language mediates and shares that degradation— the language of love no less than that of politics or "educational" (i.e., domesticating) systems:

FOR A BETTER LOVE
    "Sex is a political category" (Kate Millett)

Everyone agrees that sex
is a category in the world of lovers:
hence tenderness and its wild branches.

Everyone agrees that sex
is a category within the family:
hence children
nights together
and days apart
(he, looking for bread in the street,
in offices or factories;

she, in the rearguard of household work,
in the strategy and tactics of the kitchen
allowing them to survive in the common battle
at least until the end of the month).

Everyone agrees that sex
is an economic category:
it's enough to mention prostitution,
fashion,
sections of the newspaper for her only
or only for him.

Where the trouble begins
is the moment a woman says
sex is a political category.

Because when a woman says
sex is a political category
she can cease being woman in itself
and begin being woman for herself,
constituting the woman in woman
starting from her humanity
and not from her sex,
conscious that magical lemon-scented deodorant
and soap that voluptuously caresses her skin
are made by the same corporation that makes napalm
conscious that the tasks belonging to the home
are tasks belonging to the social class to which that home belongs,
that the difference between the sexes
shines much brighter in the deep loving night
when all those secrets that kept us
masked and strangers, become known.

       —Roque Dalton
       (Schaaf, trans.)

Our life is socially complex, specific, struggling to be realized. We need a lucid, conscious language to articulate it. Instead we're given parody complexity: complication, the surging maze. This takes many forms—such as the floating island of Laputa, with its too-familiar academy, in *Gulliver's Travels*—but all are surrounded by, rest upon, silence. Complication, the labyrinth, disorients to no end that is not a dead one. It turns only on itself. It's not harmless either, but intimately, pervasively, oppressive.

We speak the obvious or succumb to it. There *is* an obvious:

> Don't ever forget
> that the least fascist
> among the fascists
> are also
> fascists.
>> —Roque Dalton
>> (Schaaf, trans.)

authorial discretion: authoritative irresponsibility

Still there are poets who say, "I don't tell the reader what to think," as though they were making a sensitive gesture in the cause of social/political freedom and freedom of thought (not to mention preserving the miraculous autonomy of art). But no one is prisoner of a poem. Poems can be persuasive, not coercive. What *will* crimp "freedom of thought" are the desires, needs, exclusions, the fears and mystifications, constituted by the conditions under which we live and make our living.

The argument for stonewalling is self-deceiving as well as presumptuous. Poems do not exercise power as even TV ad campaigns do, or as the only newspaper in town does. Poems are not the propaganda encirclement of free speech

celebrated by the owners of the free press, who freely express
themselves and their dominion through it:

> He came to us
> and said
>
> you are not responsible
> either for the world or for the end of the world
> the burden is taken from your shoulders
> you are like birds and children
> play
>
> and they play
>
> they forget
> that modern poetry
> is a struggle for breath

> —Tadeusz Różewicz
> "The Deposition of the Burden"
> (Czesław Miłosz, trans.)

Authorial discretion, hand over mouth, seems
considerate of the reader.[4] No one gets breathed on. The
reader's "freedom" or sensibility is left intact. Yet stonewalling,
which here might be called sandbagging, renders the poet a
subject (capable of social practice) while reducing the reader
to an object (a social symptom, a thing). The reader is
projected as passive—seen, known, acted upon—whereas the
poet appropriates and reserves the privilege, to herself or
himself, of acting, seeing and knowing. Authorial discretion
assumes individual autonomy (author as transcendental
subject). That assumption is rooted in the ideology of private,
or antisocial, property, which is in its furthest reaches the
ideology of property itself.[5] Though such discretion has a
veneer of humaneness, its antisocial basis comes through in
that the humanization of some, especially of the "self," is

predicated on the dehumanization of others. The poet is person; the reader, a kind of ward. Beyond that lies the inadmissible: that "the humanization of some" is predicated on the dehumanization of all, "self" included.

Then there is the poststructuralist project. Its managed disappearance of the historically-situated subject seems opposed to the humanist project, whose "author" is sublimated from social being into a sensibility innocent of all but "self" (its innocence of ramification and consequence making it anything *but* innocent). But by desituating and dehistoricizing the work, poststructuralism ends up in line with the humanist position. The results are all too familiar. Telegraphing self-fulfillment, the work's specious authority will derive from the illusion that it is not value-bound, not historically conditioned, not responsible. Not in fact authored but "inspired": the passed-on product of a muse or maybe a "narrative," but not the production of a historically specific, socialized subject. The work's "authoritativeness" will depend not on the masking of its particular human source but on the implicit denial that it comes from anywhere at all, or that it is class-couched. The traces of production will be obliterated; the work itself, naturalized. It will *be* ideology.

Where does that leave *us*?

I must learn to hide
from my persecutors
and am thereby
in double danger

Perhaps not well enough
hidden from them
and perhaps by now
hidden too well from myself

—Erich Fried, "In Hiding"
(Stuart Hood, trans.)

tendency writing

During the last century, progressive literature associated with the Young Germany Movement was called *Tendenz,* "the tendency."[6] Defined in opposition to so-called pure art, it was also called committed writing. The significance of *Tendenzpoesie* lay in its concrete historical engagement, at least up through the Revolution of 1848. Also, *Tendenz* was practiced by associates of Marx and Engels and was commented on by those two, especially by Engels, who was critical.

The novelty of tendency writing came from its being a politically gestated "aesthetic" practice. *Tendenz* was cast in political struggle. There seems, on a superficial look-through, no precedent for it. Not the polis art of an Aeschylus wedged into philosophical fissures at the core of its world, nor the hit-and-run satire and invective in Greek and Latin literature. It doesn't match up with the moral, social satire of much 17th- and 18th-century European literature either. Nor with the decent-minded, overreaching and idealist social response of isolated, individually activist English poets, though it's tempting to make exceptions of Blake and Shelley. Are Dante and Milton precursors? Whatever, *Tendenz* was not sideline or Olympian commentary, but engagement with actual political power.

In time, *Tendenz* would refer to insistently politicized art committed to revolutionary struggle. Now the term suggests art that is engaged, didactic, and developed from a consistent political perspective, usually socialist or communist.[7] Unlike protest art, tendency art has a focused, positive aspiration— not simply a notion of social injustice, say, based on the standard-of-justice of an unjust system, but a working concept of concrete, *systemic* remedy.

realism & partisanship

Tendency art articulates latent historical tendencies. Or, to put this negatively, it's an art that refuses the harmonizing, the glossing and freeze-framing, of bourgeois ideology. *Tendenz* is as much a function of realism—not any convention of realism, but realism as revelation of, and contention with, the dynamics and ramifications of social interrelationship—as of partisanship. Realism and partisanship are inseparable. It's not simply that partisanship without realism may be toothless, but that the dependency is the other way round: there can be no realism without partisanship.[8] (We can't describe *any*thing accurately without entering into a relationship with it and accounting for that relationship in our description. This doesn't mean we must be "subjective" rather than "objective," though those are question-begging terms, but that we must struggle to be objective about our subjectivity. For instance, Yeats attempted this in his Doctrine of the Mask as well as in individual works such as "Easter 1916.") But the partisanship has to be conscious. Unconscious or unavowed partisanship is a bottomless pit, precisely the condition of "apolitical" art. In *that* there is no present, no future, no living history. Only compulsions, reactions, postures, tableaux.

form & Engels

Tendency writing cannot consist of sheer assertion. Willful partisanship is a function of idealist presumption (one of the more notorious, historically, being the idealist stance of Zhdanov). If tendency writing is to amplify and unravel contradictions informing the current growing and decaying social configuration, it has to proceed from materialist assumptions. That is also why tendency art does not prescribe formal criteria, even though it is, must be, suffused with formal considerations. The realism of tendency writing is not conceived as a particular form or style, but as social practice. This is the realism of demythification (of phenomena) and demystification (of consciousness). It owes nothing to received conventions of realism or to the parody realism of representation.[9]

Still, tendency writing has had a poor press. Engels himself, maintaining a metaphysical rather than a materialist distinction between form and content, was hostile toward it. This from one letter: "The more the opinions of the author remain hidden, the better for the work of art."

He attacked "Schillerism" as "making individuals into mere mouthpieces of the spirit of the times." Though in a late (1885) letter to Minna Kautsky he did qualify his rejection of *Tendenz:*

> I am not at all an opponent of tendentious writing as such. The father of tragedy, Aeschylus, and the father of comedy, Aristophanes, were both strong tendentious poets, as were Dante and Cervantes...But I believe the tendency must spring forth from the situation and the action itself, without explicit attention being called to it; the writer is not obliged to offer to the reader the future historical solution of the social conflicts he depicts...

To salvage something from this, Raymond Williams suggested that Engels's criticisms relate to "'applied tendency'—the mere addition of political opinions and phrases, or unrelated moral comments." In other words, the "tendency writing" that is editorialization, the fault being that it is *formally* intrusive. And it's true that Engels usually has novels or plays in mind—novels and plays, moreover, as conceived and practiced in *his* time. He objects to the tendentious violation of fictive constructions, or of the fiction conventions with which he was familiar. In this respect his opposition is based on narrowly formalist concerns. It's significant that neither he nor Marx, as far as I know, complained of the poet Heine's tendentiousness, though they did make caustic comments on its political thrust.

Some of Engels's criticism does seem based on a Romantic appeal to "organic form," but one honed by the contempt that a dedicated political activist is likely to have for politically dabbling literati. Early on (1851), referring to the Young Germany Movement, he says:

> A crude Constitutionalism, or a still cruder Republican-ism, was preached by almost all writers of the time. It became more and more the habit, particularly of the inferior sorts of literati, to make up for the want of cleverness in their productions by political allusions which were sure to attract attention. Poetry, novels, reviews, the drama, every literary production teemed with what was called "tendency," that is with more or less timid exhibitions of an antigovernment spirit.

This characterizes literature which, although *about* social or political conditions, has no penetrating social analysis and so falls short of effective social practice. Nor does the work itself constitute social practice. It is only protest literature, the groans and exclamations of an uneasy liberalism. And yet, as happens, attacks on such literature extend to tendency writing as well, caricaturing it, making it beneath comment not only for the ruling class and its cultural support system but for much of the culture-working left also, which continues to mark time in the lockups of bourgeois "aesthetics."

responsibility: from the viewpoint of production

Using terms that are unself-critical yet suggestive, Morawski calls tendency writing "the projection by essentially discursive yet poeticized means of an idea of history and of the attitudes, feelings, conflicts, *etc.* of the artistic personality (the author) about this idea." When we look at it from the inside out, we find that tendency poetry obliterates the illusion of distance between poet and poem. Not formally, but with respect to assumed responsibility. The illusory distinction between poet and poem dissolves, but does so *only from the viewpoint of production,* not necessarily from that of critical reception or consumption. For the critic there may be no poet, only a work or a boundary-shifting text. But for the poet or producer, even the producer as a socially defined "discourse-medium" rather than a metaphysically posited "source," there is social being, and some sort of self-identity, and therefore social implication and critical juncture and decision. There is responsibility.

Responsibility not only in the writing but also in the being of the writing, even when that writing is well out of hand. It remains a gesture of the producer, whatever is made of it. It's in this sense, the only meaningful sense from the perspective of production, that the tendency poet contends with values enacted by and through the work. There is no lyric washing of the hands, no signaling "don't hold me accountable for what I say and do, I'm only a symptom, or I'm only a site where saying takes place, where meaning emerges with its slow thighs to trouble the sight...I'm only saying what is, passing it on..."

responsibility: socializing experience

This does not mean that responsibility is individually determined (the miserable niche that the *moral* carves out of the *social*), or that it may be sufficiently informed by sheer personal experience.[10] Responsibility, like experience, must be socialized. Accordingly, tendentious writing would not restrict or deny personal experience but enhance and extend it. *Tendenz* begins by fulfilling the conditions of an art, referred to by Jameson and others, which prepares us to learn, really learn, by permitting us "to grasp the essentially historical and social value of what we had otherwise taken to be a question of individual experience." More significantly, tendency writing would not simply contextualize or *typify* personal experience but would expose that experience as being, of itself, an isolation pit. Personal experience, privileged, degenerates into a cultivated ignorance: another walled garden.[11]

All poetry, like language itself, is social. Open to the world. Tendency poetry takes this condition literally and seriously, as an opportunity rather than an inconvenience. An opportunity not to "preach" but to sing—to a socially rather than an individually defined someone—even if the song must often be rueful:[12]

> For $140,000
> you can scratch your back
> with Brancusi's *Bird in Space.*
>
> Just $17
> and you'll receive *Fortune* magazine
> for twelve months.
> Poor peon
> who barely makes $55 a year:
> the worth of modern sculpture
> is an unresolved matter,
> and *Fortune*
> comes out only in English,
> so why kid yourself?
>
> May eternal spring be with you, compatriot
> of our Central American soccer (junior division) champions!
>
> —Roque Dalton, "60% of El Salvador"
> (Schaaf, trans.)

This the most consciously social of poetries turns on the second person, *you*, the pronoun of intimacy and division we are given to struggle with—though its welling subtext is the collective *we* which is partly assumed, still to be realized. Of course that collectivity cannot be realized without struggle. Nor without going well beyond current political definitions and boundaries. Any tendentiousness is disturbing, even to people whose interests and values approximate those of the work itself, because it forces recognition of living issues. Issues *of* living. And that is scary.[13] Not only is struggle inescapable: in tendency poetry, struggle, largely class struggle, is declared *and* engaged.

bringing language back to life

Granted that the *materia* of social problems are already raised and defined. It does not take tendency poetry to do that. However, they are raised and defined in terms of the dominant, empowered class. Social contradictions and conflicts are mythified as symptoms of a "condition" (a fact of life, a dehistoricized situation without historic cause and therefore without remedy) rather than revealed as problematical and as socially originated (therefore actionable and solvable):

> There have been good people in this country
> ready to die for the revolution.
> But the revolution everywhere needs people
> who are ready not only to die
> but also to kill for it.
>
> About those good people Che said:
> "They are capable of dying in torture chambers
> without letting out a single word,
> but they are incapable of taking out
> a machine gun nest."

And the class enemy as is well known
uses not only torture chambers
to defend exploitation
but also machine gun nests
and all sorts of such things.

In short:
only those who are ready to die and kill
will end up being people who are good
for the revolution.

Because it's through *them* the revolution will be made.

Though the revolution ends up being for
all good people.

—Roque Dalton, "Old Communists and Guerrillas"
(Schaaf; trans.)

This is not an image-generating language. Nor does it
have the forked tongue of complication and indeterminacy.
The subtlety is in the precision, the discrimination, the
transparent respect vesting the gesture. And it is in the fine-
tuning not of the self-congratulatory obvious, but of the
unassuming: here, the prepositions:

En resumidas cuentas:
sólo aquellos que estén dispuestos a morir y matar
llegarán hasta el final siendo buenas personas
para la revolución.

Porque será por ellas que habrá revolución.

Aunque la revolución termine por ser para
todas las buenas personas.

The generative contradiction of the poem is manifest in the sibling *por* and *para* *(through/by* and *for)* that play off one another, with sly wit, down to their hospitable and remarkably gentle conclusion. The idealist assumption that what is *for* all decent people must transpire *through* them, through all such regardless—as though dehistoricized ends might constitute historical means—is stopped in midflight and seen (read) through.

Tendency poetry realizes a *lived* poetic. This is not just a matter of taking poetry seriously. Rather, here is a poetry conscious of living social context: what it is becoming and what it is coming up against. In idealist poetries the awareness of limits induces fatalism, cynicism, sentimentality. It reinforces the stupefying belief that truth is relative, that the fragments of experience cannot be added up—as they cannot be *if* experience is conceived subjectively, in isolation, rather than socially. But in tendency poetry the encounter with limits *is* an encounter. It produces historical specificity. The fact is that truth isn't relative, it's historical. This isn't something that can be learned. We have to keep on learning it. *Truth is not relative, it's historical.* It is arrived at through personal social struggle. There are no shortcuts. The almost transpersonal optimism of tendency poetry flows from the understanding that there are no truths, not even scientific ones, that are not historically conditioned.

How assume otherwise? How assume that poetry may be exempt from the historicity of its, and our, world? All language is of life, social life. It's remarkable how little curiosity many poets have regarding their own language. How much they give up on, and how readily. There's interest in deracinated etymology, in words "untimely ripped," but little or none in the concrete historical content of the language they use, nor in its social function. Nor in whose language it is.

Render unto God the things that are God's
and unto the fascist government of President Molina
what belongs to the fascist government of Pres. Molina.

I don't pretend to know, from my limited perspective,
all that belongs to God

but, yes, I'm sure about what we ought to give
the fascist government of Molina.

> —Roque Dalton
> from "Variations on a Phrase by Christ"
> (Schaaf, trans.)

tendency poetry imperfect

Tendency poetry assumes a present not sealed off, like one
time capsule addressed to another, but activated with the
reader. Rather than close on itself like an archive, where life is
congealed, object-ified, no longer becoming, it *enacts*
socialization. That's why tendency poems are not self-
contained but generative. They hang around, resist being
finished off:[14]

ARS POETICA 1974

Poetry
pardon me for having helped you to understand
you are not made of words alone.

> —Roque Dalton
> (Schaaf, trans.)

Tendency poetry would not simply manifest social being.
It would constitute, and be constituted by, social transaction.
From the perspective of production, tendency poets and

poetries are especially obliged to look and listen, because "the world" goes on talking back, surrounding and impressing, returning the challenge posed by Rilke's archaic torso of Apollo and demanding that the poet (poetry) change his or her life and understanding of life and "art." Here's Brecht on a lesson learned from workers/actors staging *Die Massnahme* (*The Measures Taken*):

> The workers judged everything according to the truth of its content; they welcomed every innovation which helped the representation of truth, of the real mechanisms of society...Anything that was worn out, trivial, or so commonplace that it no longer made one think, they did not like at all ("you get nothing out of it"). If one needed an aesthetic, one could find it here. I shall never forget how a worker looked at me when I replied to his suggestion that I should add something to a chorus about the Soviet Union ("It has got to go in—otherwise what's the point?"), that it would destroy the artistic form. He put his head on one side and smiled. A whole area of aesthetics collapsed because of his polite smile. The workers are not afraid to teach us and they were not themselves afraid to learn.[15]

Tendency poetry is risky. Even subjectivity and self-identity (or self-misrecognition) are at hazard:

THE PETTY BOURGEOISIE
    (one of its manifestations)

Those who
in most cases
want to make revolution
for History for logic
for science and nature
for next year's books or the future
to win arguments and even
to appear finally in the newspapers

and not simply
to put an end to the hunger
of those who are hungry
and the exploitation
of those who are exploited.

It is natural, then,
that in revolutionary practice
they only concede before the judgment of History
morality humanism logic science
books and newspapers
and refuse to concede the last word
to the hungry the exploited
who have their own history of horror
their own implacable logic
and who will have their own books
their own science
nature
and future

—Roque Dalton
(Schaaf, trans.)

tendency & socialist realism

Tendency poetry entails the realism of demystification and demythification, not of representation.[16] Which is why tendency poetry doesn't hole up, becoming merely one kind of form (i.e., a style). It engages becoming.

Socialist realism was also supposed to engage becoming. That potential was squelched: by the revolutionary romanticism, if we may call it that, proclaimed by Zhdanov— a romanticism so utopian that even he had to insist it was not; by the inertia of a bourgeois past, which was also a present, and by the demands of a politically temporizing present, a future-dominated present, whereby the frontier fluidity of proletarian internationalism was being displaced by a united front of (static, bourgeois) nationalisms. Socialist realism flaked off into the sorry thing characterized by Trotsky in the late Thirties: "The 'realism' consists in the imitation of provincial daguerreotypes of the third quarter of the last century; the 'socialist' character apparently consists in representing, in the manner of pretentious photography, events which never took place." The potential of socialist realism now goes unrecognized, if not unrealized, though some of the more mature 20th-century poetry follows from the philosophical (not, repeat, the historically effected) bases of socialist realist art.[17]

The Turkish poet Nazim Hikmet went so far as to use socialist realist principle to question the stultifying exoskeleton that socialist realism had become historically.

I have some questions for the cosmonauts
did they see the stars much larger
were they like huge jewels on black velvet
                    or apricots on orange
does it make a person feel proud to get a little closer to the stars
I saw color photos of the cosmos in Ogonek magazine now don't get
          upset comrades but nonfigurative shall we say or abstract
          well some of them looked just like such paintings which is
          to say they were terribly figurative and concrete
my heart was in my mouth looking at them
they are the endlessness of our longing to grasp things
looking at them I could think even of death and not feel one bit sad
I never knew I loved the cosmos
               —Nazim Hikmet
               "Things I Didn't Know I Loved"
               (Randy Blasing and Mutlu Konuk, trans.)

The poem is dated April 1962, when such issues were being aired. Seven or eight months later Khrushchev made his notorious attack, at the scene of a Moscow art exhibit, on nonfigurative or "modernist" tendencies in Soviet art.

partisan poetry & party poetry

It has been noted that tendency poetry is partisan poetry.[18] Certainly all literature is partisan, a compounding of interests, perspectives, class values, ends. But tendency poetry acknowledges its partisanship. It does not make a virtue of being at the mercy of unconscious bias (though no poetry or language, including this one, escapes that entirely). Still, partisanship is one thing. Lenin's *partiinost*, "party-spirited" literature, is something else: an extension of partisanship, but so intensified in degree that it becomes different in kind. The questions raised by *partiinost* are provocative, not least because they are bound up with the necessities of revolutionary transformation. Serious, prolonged struggle requires organization and discipline. There's no way around that. The question, which for us in the U.S. still awaits an answer, is, what kind of organization? Discipline how constituted?

Tendentious literature does not have to be party-spirited literature. Usually it is not. But what happens when it is? Problems arise when "party-spirited" cools into "party-outlined"—when the literature is abstracted in accord with ephemeral aspects of a policy that at any given moment must be, no matter how hard it tries not to be, blindly literal.[19] And so, blind to itself and its consequences...more attuned to tactics than to strategy. Or mistaking the relationship between them. That will happen, of course. That's the chance taken by any movement or organization engaged in revolutionary struggle. Yet that same chance has also to be taken *by* literature and, as regards revolutionary organizations, *with* literature. There has to be that good faith. Brecht had something of the sort in mind when he accused Lukács and others of being "enemies of production": "Production makes them uncomfortable. You never know where you are with production; production is unforeseeable. You never know what's going to come out. And they themselves don't want to produce. They want to play the *apparatchik* and exercise control over other people. Every one of their criticisms contains a threat."

CROCK LOGIC

"Criticism of the Soviet Union
can only be made by one who is anti-Soviet.

Criticism of China
can only be made by one who is anti-China.

Criticism of the Salvadoran Communist Party
can only be made by an agent of the CIA.

Self-criticism is equivalent to suicide."

—Roque Dalton
(Schaaf, trans.)

Party-spirited literature is written in free association with a party or it is nothing, least of all effective. It must be produced by party-committed human beings, not functionaries. But this is a problem to be worked out by those who have the experience and competence to do so. The issue may not seem pressing now, when local revolutionary organizations are weak and undeveloped. But sooner or later there will be no way around it. History tends to eliminate options, or the illusion of options. (Objectively. Subjectively, as we've seen, that illusion can be carried into the teeth of any reality.) There will have to be a party-spirited literature. Not the literature of ad hoc or issue-bound groups—which are theoretically and practically self-incapacitating—but of fundamentally principled, ultimately mass-revolutionary organizations. At some point it should be clear that there are no sidelines to stand back of: no "aesthetic" area sealed off from a "political," no knowing apart from doing, no moral values dissociated from actual conduct:

DEATH CERTIFICATE

"Because it's all no use
They do as they please anyhow

Because I don't want to get
my fingers burnt again

Because they'll just laugh:
it only needed you!

And why always me?
I'll get no thanks for it

Because no one can sort this out
One might only make things worse

Because even what's bad
may have some good in it

Because it depends on how you look at it
and anyway whom can you trust?

Because the other side too
gets wet when it rains

Because I'd rather leave it
to those more qualified

Because you never know
what you let yourself in for

Because it's a waste of effort
They don't deserve it"

These are the causes of death
to write on our graves

which will not even be dug
if these are the causes

—Erich Fried
(Georg Rapp, trans.)

So, tendency poetry. Or something of it. The case of *Tendenz* needs to be reconsidered, especially by those developing a language adequate to engage it. There's already enough tendency poetry to support such an undertaking.[20] An undertaking, note, that has been denigrated and suppressed for the very reasons that revolutionary parties have been put down (not piecemeal, relative to weaknesses or questionable policies, but categorically, in their entirety): because they cannot be pocketed or otherwise contained. They are systemically subversive practices.

1. At the time this was written, two translated selections of Dalton's poetry were about to come out: *Poems* (Willimantic, Ct.: Curbstone Press, 1984), translated by Richard Schaaf, and *Clandestine Poems / Poemas Clandestinos* (San Francisco: Solidarity Publications, 1984), translated by Jack Hirschman. Appropriately, money to help publish the latter was raised through a community activists' dance in the Mission district of San Francisco.

2. Granted that a saying or a writing "signifies" in more ways than one, and that no one wraps this up. Granted too that what we think means more than we realize, and that (language being historical) what we say means more and less than we intend, and that meaning does not entirely preexist but is produced also in the saying. But 'meaning' in that sense is not at issue here. What is is what happens as we exercise intentions and are, in consequence, socially accountable. Any discourse is specifically produced. There must be a producer. The question is *where* the producing, the speaking, is from.

    In certain respects the assumptions of this discussion are untenable. It's not possible to have a thought independent of the language realizing it, nor independent of the social context where that language is played out, and whereby that language is itself in part constituted. But this only means that thought, however intimate or fleeting, is socially constituted.

3. A silence that, in a prefatory, tellingly aestheticized show of power, exposes itself as thick, unbroken, coldly palpable. In context the silence materializes not as an "it" but as "he" who

    > toward Eve
    > Addressed his way, not with indented wave
    > Prone on the ground, as since, but on his rear,
    > Circular base of rising folds, that towered
    > Fold above fold a surging maze; his head
    > Crested aloft, and carbuncle his eyes;
    > With burnished neck of verdant gold, erect
    > Amidst his circling spires, that on the grass
    > Floated redundant...

4. It hardly matters whether the text is "written" or "spoken," or whether a critic may divine an author behind, or describe an author produced by, the text. This discussion is of the production of texts from the perspective, the subject-position, of the immediate producers of texts. It's irrelevant whether authorial self-identification is achievable, or that self-identification must necessarily be self-misrecognition. Though self-identity is problematical in that it is social, historical— ever a *becoming*—the fact is, every producer does adopt, conceive, or misconceive a functionally effective identity.

5. The notion of a process whereby one is liberated from the condition of an "object" (seen, known, acted upon) so as to assume the condition of a "subject" (seeing, knowing, acting upon) has been engaging and useful. Nonetheless it has been criticized, partly on the grounds that its positing of a "self" is metaphysical. There is also the criticism that *any* concept of self is a concept of property, and so must necessarily constitute human relations as property relations (witness the "love" songs on the pop music charts). Yet such criticism often replaces that self or subject with an easily paradoxical "decentered subject" which is itself metaphysical and corresponds, politically, to liberal ideology. One may be everywhere, and has to be nowhere. *Has to* be nowhere.

6. The Young Germany Movement was liberal, nationalist, constitutionalist. The general push was for a German national state with a representative assembly. This meant, of course, opposition to divine right. On a popular level there was also opposition to medieval restrictions on apprentices, artisans and peasants. The intellectuals agitated for free speech and trial by jury.

7. For this and other reasons it makes no sense to include someone like the Greek poet Cavafy—whose considerable work is often tendentious and socially dimensioned—as a tendency poet. Nor, say, the 17th-century poet George Herbert, who beneath a transparency of dramatic meditation is remarkably persistent in pressing a religiously ideological (smoothing over, harmonizing) tendentiousness.

8. "All of our descriptive statements move within an often invisible network of value-categories...It is not just as though we have something called factual knowledge which may then be distorted by particular interests and judgments, although this is certainly possible; it is also that without particular interests we would have no knowledge at all...Interests are *constitutive* of our knowledge, not merely prejudice which imperils it. The claim that knowledge should be 'value-free' is itself a value-judgment." Terry Eagleton, *Literary Theory, An Introduction* (Minneapolis: University of Minnesota Press, 1983), 14.

    In *Reception Theory: A Critical Introduction* (New York: Methuen, 1984), Robert C. Holub summarizes Hans-Georg Gadamer's extension of Heidegger's rethinking of being. "While previous theory had advocated a purging of preconceptions, Heidegger claims that it is precisely our being-in-the-world with its prejudices and presuppositions that makes understanding possible...Gadamer takes up this issue most thoroughly in his discussion of prejudice [*Vorurteil*]. The word in German, like its English equivalent, although etymologically related to prejudging or merely forming a judgment about something beforehand, has come to mean a negative bias or a quality that excludes accurate judgment. The enlightenment, Gadamer claims, is responsible for this discrediting of the notion of prejudice. But this discrediting, he continues, is itself the result of a prejudice that is linked to the methodological claims to truth proposed by the natural sciences. Prejudice, because it belongs to historical reality itself, is not a hindrance to understanding, but rather a condition of the possibility of understanding" (pp. 40-41).

For a related, "politicized" view, read the comments on prediction, impartiality and partisanship in Antonio Gramsci's *Selections from the Prison Notebooks* (New York: International Publishers, 1971), 170-72.

9. Not the stagnant, flattened "realism" of idealist thought, but the demystifying realism of dialectical materialism. It has become fashionable to pass over dialectical materialism, or to dismiss it without having the vaguest notion as to what it might (rightly or wrongly) mean. To the ancient Greeks, "dialectics" meant disclosing contradictions in an opponent's argument. But for Lenin dialectics is "the splitting of a single whole and the cognition of its contradictory parts." What in nature or society seems a homogeneous whole contains internal contradictions. It is by means of (not in spite of) these contradictions, struggling oppositions, that the seemingly stable whole develops and is transformed.

Among Marxists there are differing interpretations and applications of the term. What's more, dialectical materialism may be deconstructed (provided the deconstructor, assuming a liberal position, levitates). Nonetheless even raw generalizations indicate something of its richness and power. Dialectical materialism is defined in opposition to metaphysical idealism. The basic assumptions of the dialectical *method*, as schematized under Stalin's name, are: a) that everything is an interconnected and integral whole; b) that everything in the world is in a state of continuous movement and change; c) that imperceptible quantitative changes at some point become qualitative (i.e., categorical) ones; and d) that contradiction is inherent in all things. These contrast with idealist assumptions: a) that things are unconnected and independent of each other; b) that nature is basically immutable; c) that process is a simple development of growth, wherein quantitative changes never become qualitative ones; and d) that contradictions, if any, are among things rather than within them.

Historical materialism extends the principles of dialectical materialism to the study of social life. These are the terms of the realism we speak of in connection with tendency poetry.

10. The question is, what constitutes "personal experience"? What *is* such experience actually *of?* As Raymond Williams points out, "Ideology...is very much more than the ideas and beliefs of particular

classes or groups. It is in effect, with only limited exceptions, the condition of all conscious life. Thus the area to which most students of literature normally refer their reading and their judgment, that area summarized in the decisive term 'experience,' has in fact to be seen as within the sphere of ideology. Indeed, experience is seen as the most common form of ideology. It is where the deep structures of the society actually reproduce themselves as conscious life." Raymond Williams, "Crisis in English Studies," *Writing in Society* (London: Verso, n.d.), 207.

11. The privileging of individual personal experience has led to, or abetted, the marked visual-reference bias of so much modern poetry in English. Fetishized visual phenomena represent, project, a sense-bound version of the "concrete" or substantial. As one dissenting theorist remarks: "The apparently concrete, the text, turns out, on further inspection, to be an abstraction whereas the apparently abstract, the system of relationships between texts, proves to be the concrete or, more accurately, a necessary abstraction through which it is alone possible to encounter the text in its particular, determinate and historically varying concrete forms. The concrete, Marx remarks in the *Grundrisse,* is the result and not the point of departure for thought." Tony Bennett, *Formalism and Marxism* (New York: Methuen, 1979), 175.

A similar observation is made by Michael Ryan: "The semblance of 'being as presence'—a perceptible plenitude in the present moment—is thus simply an effect of complex chains of relations whose texture is never 'present' as such. As Marx would have put it, had he lived to be a critic of phenomenology, to privilege perception is to limit oneself to 'things,' at the expense of the imperceptible social relations that produce them." Michael Ryan, *Marxism and Deconstruction* (Baltimore: Johns Hopkins University Press, 1982), 22.

The fetishizing of sensory experience and of "things" has its broad rationale in empiricism. But traces of this bias (which having broken through one superstition has, in time, become a succeeding superstition) are evident even in the limited course of modern American poetry. E.g., William Carlos Williams: "...what actually impinges on the senses must be rendered as it appears, by use of which, only, and under which, untouched, the significance has to be disclosed. It is one of the major problems of the artist." Despite some hedging, the first Imagist principle—"direct treatment of the 'thing' whether subjective or objective"—underwrites the same priority, with its assumption of a transparent or self-canceling language. At the aesthetic extreme, the poem itself is fetishized, as in MacLeish's metaphysically materialist "A poem should not mean / But be," at which point the social silence is deafening.

Pursuing the matter we find that the roots of this empiricist bias are not materialist, as might be assumed, but idealist. The drive is toward *dehistoricized* being. The attempt is to render the *dehistoricized* 'thing.' Not incidentally, it is also an attempt to purge language ("to purify the dialect of the tribe"), to free it from the implication of history. The following passage, from an article on photography, is suggestive: "E. H. Gombrich has traced the lineage of the belief in the ineffable purity of the visual image. Plato puts into the mouth of Socrates a doctrine of two worlds: the world of murky imperfection to which our mortal senses have access; and an 'upper world' of perfection and light. *Discursive speech is the tangled and inept medium to which we are condemned in the former* [my italics], while in the latter all things are communicated visually as a pure and unmediated intelligibility which has no need for words. The idea that there are two quite distinct forms of communication, words and images, and that the latter is the more direct, passed via the Neo-Platonists into the Christian tradition. There was now held to be a divine language of *things,* richer than the language of words; those who apprehend the difficult but divine truths enshrined in things do so in a flash, without the need for words and arguments. As Gombrich observes, such traditions 'are of more than antiquarian interest. They still affect the way we talk and think about the art of our own time.'" Victor Burgin, "Photography, Phantasy, Function," *Thinking Photography* (London: Macmillan, 1982), 214.

What's "wrong" with discursive language, with speech itself, is that it is historical. (We may detect an affiliated bias in current attempts to privilege Lacan's prelinguistic "mirror phase.") The impulse that promoted, in photography, the "ineffable purity of the visual [i.e., nondiscursive] image" coincided ideologically and to some extent historically with the Imagist impulse (in fact reaction) to minimize or repress discursive language in favor of "things" or "images." Considering what those and allied aesthetics exclude—a Wilfred Owen, for instance, despite his sensuous "imaging"—it's not difficult to figure their social function.

12. "Every literary text is built out of a sense of its potential audience, includes an image of whom it is written *for:* every work encodes within itself what Iser calls an 'implied reader,' intimates in its every gesture the kind of 'addressee' it anticipates…It is not just that a writer 'needs an audience': the language he uses already implies one range of possible audiences rather than another." Eagleton, 84.

13. "Nothing about the problems of Negroes was ever taught in the classrooms at school; and whenever I would raise these questions with the boys, they would either remain silent or turn the subject into a joke. They were vocal about the petty individual wrongs they suffered,

but they possessed no desire for a knowledge of the picture as a whole. Then why was I worried about it?" Richard Wright, *Black Boy.*

14. Walter Benjamin links the "unfinished character" of such work with the necessity of changing the production apparatus rather than simply providing grist for its mill. I quote at length because his modest, companionable subtlety is helpful in ways that cannot be summarized. He notes that Brecht "was the first to address to the intellectuals the far-reaching demand that they should not supply the production apparatus without, at the same time, within the limits of the possible, changing that apparatus in the direction of Socialism. 'The publication of the *Versuche*,' we read in [Brecht's] introduction to the series of texts published under that title, 'marks a point at which certain works are not so much intended to represent individual experiences (i.e. to have the character of finished works) as they are aimed at using (transforming) certain existing institutes and institutions.'...Here I should like to confine myself to pointing out the decisive difference between merely supplying a production apparatus and changing it...To supply a production apparatus without trying, within the limits of the possible, to change it, is a highly disputable activity even when the material supplied appears to be of a revolutionary nature. For we are confronted with the fact—of which there has been no shortage of proof over the last decade [*Benjamin presented this paper in 1934*]—that the bourgeois apparatus of production and publication is capable of assimilating, indeed of propagating, an astonishing amount of revolutionary themes without ever seriously putting into question its own continued existence or that of the class which owns it. In any case this remains true so long as it is supplied by hacks, albeit revolutionary hacks. And I define a hack as a man who refuses as a matter of principle to improve the production apparatus and so prise it away from the ruling class for the benefit of Socialism. I further maintain that an appreciable part of so-called left-wing literature had no other social function than that of continually extracting new effects or sensations from this situation for the public's entertainment...

"I have spoken of the way in which [the New Objectivity, a literary movement] has turned *the struggle against misery* into an object of consumption...The characteristic feature of this literature is the way it transforms political struggle so that it ceases to be a compelling motive for decision and becomes an object of comfortable contemplation; it ceases to be a means of production and becomes an article of consumption...

"An author who has carefully thought about the conditions of production today...will never be concerned with products alone, but always, at the same time, with the means of production. In other words, his products must possess an organizing function besides and before their character as finished works. And their organizational usefulness must on no account be confined to propagandistic use. Commitment alone will not do it…The best opinion is of no use if it does not make something useful of those who hold it. The best 'tendency' is wrong if it does not prescribe the attitude with which it ought to be pursued. And the author can only prescribe such an attitude in the place where he is active, that is to say in his writing. Commitment is a necessary, but never a sufficient, condition for a writer's work acquiring an organizing function. For this to happen it is also necessary for the writer to have a teacher's attitude…*A writer who does not teach other writers teaches nobody.* The crucial point, therefore, is that a writer's production must have the character of a model: it must be able to instruct other writers in their production and, second, it must be able to place an improved apparatus at their disposal. This apparatus will be the better, the more consumers it brings in contact with the production process—in short, the more readers or spectators it turns into collaborators." *Reflections* (New York: Harcourt Brace Jovanovich, 1978), 220-238.

15. The identification of dehistoricized "form" (codified or prescribed style) with "quality" has been one of the more effective ploys in securing, philosophically at least, ruling class cultural hegemony as regards the arts.

    In one of his talks at the Yenan Forum, Mao Zedong outlined a class-cognizant, historically grounded approach to the issue of "artistic" quality: "We must popularize only what is needed and can be readily accepted by the workers, peasants and soldiers themselves. Consequently, prior to the task of educating the workers, peasants and soldiers, there is the task of learning from them. This is even more true of raising standards. There must be a basis from which to raise…From what basis, then, are literature and art to be raised? From the basis of the feudal classes? From the basis of the bourgeoisie? From the basis of the petit bourgeois intellectuals? No, not from any of these; only from the basis of the masses of workers, peasants and soldiers. Nor does this mean raising the workers, peasants and soldiers to the 'heights' of the feudal classes, the bourgeoisie or the petit bourgeois intellectuals; it means raising the level of literature and art in the direction in which the workers, peasants and soldiers are themselves advancing, in the direction in which the proletariat is advancing. Here again the task of learning from the workers, peasants and soldiers comes in." Mao Zedong, "Talks at the Yenan Forum on Literature and Art" in *Mao Tse-tung on Literature and Art* (Peking: Foreign Languages Press, 1967), 16-17.

    The authors of a recent article on cultural policy in Sandinista Nicaragua also break the ideological linkage between prescribed, dehistoricized "form" and quality: "Since they are premised on an awareness of how historical self-consciousness is a precondition for cultural self-determination, the advances in Nicaraguan art have necessarily gone beyond formalism, because formalism is, above all, historical ignorance raised to the level of an aesthetic principle. Mainstream notions of aesthetic 'quality' in the United States and Europe—which largely isolate art forms from history and then fetishize those forms as all-important, with a few concluding remarks about the 'ineffability' of 'good taste'—are transparently self-contradictory to those who are recovering from historical amnesia, not to mention the political and economic causes of it. Hence 'quality' in the visual arts, far from being ignored, has been detrivialized by the Nicaraguans to mean something much more complex than self-serving remarks about 'good taste.'" David Craven and John Ryder, "Nicaragua's Revolution in Culture," *Arts*, January 1984.

16. What this might entail beyond our present political context remains to be seen. In *Literature and Propaganda* (New York: Methuen, 1983), A. P. Foulkes notes that "a demystifying art…is by its nature a subversive and questioning art. It challenges habits and modes of perception, and produces new ways of seeing and interpreting processes and relationships. To do this successfully, it must be unpredictable, surprising, even shocking, and it must be inventive enough to avoid being submerged by an integration propaganda which will naturalize its techniques in the guise of reproducing them" (p. 56). He also cautions that "newly established post-revolutionary sciences, whose integration propaganda tends to be clumsy and authoritarian, will usually react with hostility towards a literature which seems capable of producing this demystifying consciousness, as opposed to works which specifically expose the false consciousness resulting from capitalism" (p. 59).

17. For a standard but adequate characterization of socialist realist art, see Moisei Kagan's "The Formation and Development of Socialist Art" in *Socialist Realism in Literature and Art* (Moscow: Progress Publishers, 1971) 56-178.

18. See Lukács's 1932 essay "Tendency or Partisanship?" in *Essays on Realism*, R. Livingston, ed. (London: Lawrence & Wishart, 1980), 33-44. Although he prefers the term "partisanship" to "tendency" (the latter he considers compromised by idealist, undialectical, bourgeois origins), Lukács gives a tenable account of the interdependence of "a correct dialectical depiction of reality" and "partisanship," the latter being a precondition for such a depiction. But he is sharper in exposing the roots of the split between the Marxist sense of the word—"tendency" as social development *itself* made conscious by the

poet—and the so-called tendency which is merely subjective "desire" on the part of the author.

19. For a different interpretation of Lenin's intended application of *partiinost* to literature, see Ernst Fischer's *Art Against Ideology* (New York: Braziller, 1969), 176-82. "Lenin's demand for party-mindedness was not meant to apply to literature in general but to political writings...[According to Krupskaya] Lenin's articles *On Proletarian Culture, Party Organization and Party Literature* and *The Tasks of the Youth Leagues* do not concern literature as a fine art."

20. See *Bertolt Brecht: Poems 1913-1956*, John Willet and Ralph Manheim, eds., with Erich Fried (New York: Methuen, 1976), the best-translated, most comprehensive collection of Brecht's poetry. Four fine collections of poems by Nazim Hikmet, translated by Randy Blasing and Mutlu Konuk, are *Things I Didn't Know I Loved* (1975), *The Epic of Sheik Bedreddin* (1977), *Human Landscapes* (1982) and *Selected Poetry* (1986), all published by Persea. A smaller, earlier selection of Hikmet's poems, *The Moscow Symphony*, was translated by Taner Baybars (Chicago: Swallow, 1970). By the Polish poet Tadeusz Różewicz there are *The Survivor and Other Poems*, translated by Magnus J. Krynski and Robert A. Maguire (Princeton: Princeton University Press, 1976) and *Conversation with the Prince, and Other Poems*, translated by Adam Czerniawski (London: Anvil, 1982). A strong selection of poems by Erich Fried, *100 Poems Without a Country*, has been translated by Stuart Hood (New York: Red Dust, 1980). A selection of earlier poems by Fried, *On Pain of Seeing*, was translated by Georg Rapp (Chicago: Swallow, 1969). The work of other poets also helps focus and extend the issues raised here: e.g., that of Ernesto Cardenal, Otto René Castillo, Leonel Rugama, Javier Heraud, Alejandro Romualdo, Nicolás Guillén, René Depestre, Kim Chi Ha, Mahmoud Darwish, Sidney Sepamla, and others. It would be well to reconsider—seriously, respectfully, not through the mind-boggling prism of anticommunism—the much-patronized Mayakovsky, and to develop a critical language that will do justice to the less romanticized, more tendentious works of Neruda and, especially, to the mythified *and* mystified Vallejo.

99

REVIEW

a graphics intervention in South Africa

1

That this book was attempted is no small thing.* The limitations make it no less dedicated or passionate, even though its passion flails. What might have been intensity sheers off into monochromatic expressionism, self-absorbed where it should be attentive. There's little room for the exuberant resistance admitted by the South African Minister of Justice, who complained of courtroom demonstrations in which supporters of the accused "take up their seats...The accused then enter the hall singing and with clenched fists, take their places in the dock, and, standing, turn to the audience, whereupon all of them sing inflammatory songs...Only when the tumult has subsided can the court's session commence. When the hearing is adjourned, the accused and the audience all leave the courtroom singing, and supporters frequently continue their activities outside."[1] *Suicide* has no iconography, no terms, for resilience or for recognizing, let alone conducting, the struggle these people are engaged in. Yet there is much to be learned from the book, above all from its failings.

2

Suicide is a black book. Not racially, but in its ambiance. It is impossible to overstress this. What red there is leaks away, stains torture hands. Red is blood waste, not blood coloring and vivifying banners with the human cost of hope and

* *How to Commit Suicide in South Africa*, by Sue Coe and Holly Metz (New York: Raw Books & Graphics, 1983)

struggle. Even the red is black. Black is beginning, middle, end—obliterating history in one blind raging retina flash. There's no light, only patches where the blackness has been (momentarily) scraped away. We make out darkened figures in a darkness. That's it. But what is the darkness of? For whom is the book made? Whom does it address?

The logic of *Suicide* demands victims. If black South Africans were not defined almost exclusively as victims, so the subtextual reasoning goes, they'd have less claim on our sentimental humanitarian support (support given to death squad victims, as in El Salvador, but begrudged or denied those who win out over their oppressors, however precarious the triumph, as in Nicaragua). Certainly, to show them resisting need not detract from their status as victims. It would however leave us less free to sympathize on *dehistoricized* moral grounds. We'd have to side with their resistances, approve acts that really do damage the machinery of apartheid, and so become historically implicated. We'd have to assent to an ethic that would be tenable *within* their living struggle. Assenting, as well, to the violence that any liberation movement entails, aware that such violence is not commensurate with, nor independent of, systemic violence: the ongoing, literal mass murder that flows from the administration of exploitation. Yet the blank, indiscriminate dehistoricizing of *Suicide* makes all violence bad. Consequently only violence against the oppressed may be acknowledged.[2] The artist is stuck: confirming and reinforcing victimization, unable to admit to, never mind celebrate, the concrete struggle to destroy the system that produces such stultifying misery. The artist/authors may not have meant to end up with so bleak a book. Nonetheless their ideological assumptions, particularly as inscribed in the graphics, lead to that. And do so despite the fact that no one who hates apartheid (what other emotion is appropriate?), or who has made the commitment these cultural workers have in making this book, could have felt at ease with the frustration and defeat that speak through it.

3

The friend who brought this *Life*-sized book to my attention compared it in power and effect to the photomontages of John Heartfield. It is more reminiscent of Heartfield's co-worker George Grosz, whose memorable images, adapted from children's drawings and toilet graffiti, begin and end in gut sentiment. They're reactive. Instead of seeing *into* predatory relationships, he projects and mythifies them; he envisions social deformation in terms of misanthropic sexuality environed by *lumpen* threat and mutilation. The bourgeoisie mythified as 'philistines' can only be denied.[3] That is, Grosz seldom manages to be critical, to produce a constructive negation. There is no positive option. A similar impasse confronts *Suicide*. Without a critically mature understanding, the artist is unable to conceive a form adequate to the occasion: the exploitation and systemic repression of the black people of southern Africa. This is not a political shortcoming only, but an aesthetic one. The bold graphics, which might have been signs of life, are shadows of it...symptoms, incapable of independent development. Which is to say, they are ideological formations. They go nowhere on their own.

It should be emphasized that while Coe's graphics exude powerlessness, the text does not. The problem is that the graphics override the text, in effect *becoming* the book. And though the graphics-defined book sympathizes with the victims of apartheid, it does not assume their perspective. The work is too preoccupied with its own feelings and terms to take on the vision demanded by such identification. It remains helpless and apart. Helpless *because* apart. The graphics bespeak menace, fear, desolation. The book has the feel of a nightmare committed to paper.

4

The text, then, does not hold its own. Any reader will have a hard time making out the print—a sans serif white drop-out from encroaching blackness—but only a determined reader could salvage that text from the visual ideology occluding it. Were we to abstract the text from its visual context we'd misrepresent the practice it constitutes, making it seem to accomplish more than it does. Even so, the text deserves consideration. Apartheid after all is not a piece of legislation or a barbarism of the genes. Nor a sadism. It is a historically specific strategy for exploitation.

The text dates the populating and colonizing of southern Africa and the introduction of apartheid. Press clippings reflect, from a distance, the working lives and the oppression of black people in South Africa. The most inspiring news item is ignored by the graphics. Dated 21 September 1981, it reads:

> Workers detained, according to Ciskei Police Chief Charles Sebe, for "singing freedom songs, denouncing the present system of government, upholding a Mandela-type government [non-apartheid], and waving black power salutes." On the way back to their home in Mdstano after a meeting in East London, workers' buses were stopped and diverted to a police station, where the singing began.

Such straightforward reports are rare. Because of a tendency to hole up in press documentation and quotation— quotes come from apartheid-upholding sources, or from outside the struggle—the text itself, regardless of the authors' intention, assumes an indifferent or negative posture toward resistance. The entry dated 26 May 1982 notes that "last year was the second worst year for strikes in South African history since the black miners' strike of 1946, Parliament said yesterday." But from our perspective, the perspective of any who support those workers in their struggle, 1981 was not the second worst for strikes. It was the second *best*. Not that strikes aren't a hardship—they surely are—but that they signal resistance and hope. 'Fight back' is salutary, frightening, humanly beautiful. It disrupts the harmonious workings of systemic exploitation and repression. Only within the terms and values of that system could those strikes be condemned.

The text does nonetheless observe resistances. What doesn't is the graphics, which overpower and refuse to admit much of that text. The one clear exception is the newspaper photo of a black Ford Company worker, fist raised, during a 1981 strike over the demotions of two union leaders. Though the book does not register such distinctions, the strike dealt with workers' solidarity rather than with simple economic issues. Still, that's the least of what is overlooked. In the accompanying graphic we can hardly make out the picketers shrunk deep into the background. The foreground figures are: one black, stripped to the waist, backed exhausted up against a wall of blackness; another on the ground, apparently shot, hovered over by a slit-eyed guard; another guard, hooded, with a rifle slung over his shoulder. The footline says BLACK MUSCLE, BLACK THREAT, but the graphic doesn't take that seriously. The outstanding headline proclaims, in red, STRIKER SHOT. Indeed that is the message informing the graphic.

Even without being overshadowed by the graphics, the text comes up short on occasion. There's a page on young criminals called 'tsotsis' (said here to be a revised pronunciation of 'zoot-suiters') who prey on fellow blacks. The text implies that they lack racial solidarity, which may be so, but the example given—tsotsis robbing a migrant worker of his painfully saved wages—exposes a more devastating lack of class consciousness. Tsotsis are *lumpen*, a hovering antisocial fringe consisting of those who, atomized by the pressure of ongoing social crisis and oppression, have become 'declassed.' In effect they are not only symptoms but living instances of social disintegration. The text does not realize this, however, and makes no attempt to put the example into perspective. We're left with the insinuative, troubling image of poor young blacks mugging a poor black transient worker. Not that this doesn't happen. What's arbitrary is that the text drops the matter there, in the impacted descent of self-degradation, precisely where it would be left in the flatly ideological pages of a V. S. Naipaul. There might have been a more truthful presentation. Clearly something else exists in the world. It's not just that we have Fanon and others to elucidate the sources and dynamics of such self-destructive, profoundly antisocial behavior among segments of any oppressed population. On the positive side some of those same elements, given the opportunity to do so, enact their rage in socially positive ways. Current demonstrations reveal a long-standing, powerful mass consciousness of common interests. And the commonality is an extensive one. Indian and 'colored' boycotts of so-called new constitutional elections were not based simply on narrow racial interests. Now rebellious blacks attack not only white authorities and properties but those of the minuscule black bourgeoisie enriched by complicity with the South African government. Black policemen are also targeted. Not that all this should be spelled out in the book—it could not and should not be—but the struggle goes beyond what is conceivable within the terms of the book. Moreover, what was left out was *not* due to insufficient data or information, nor to deliberate omissions. Suppressions have been determined by the ideology informing the book, in particular by the mythicizing that selects the graphic perceptions and dictates their terms.

5

The ideology of *Suicide* shows most clearly in the mythification of dogs and of male genitalia, and in the routine manipulation of religious symbology.

Suicide is a dog-ridden nightmare.[4] Dogs in the text are doomed: "In 1977, a new black nationalist song arose: 'Zinga Zobulawa'—the dogs will be killed." In the graphics, though, they lunge, snarl, tear at. Surging into the physiognomies of South African police they become boar-like, bat-like, dinosaurian and 'evil empire' heads with needle teeth.[5] Not one is killed. But how could it be? The dogs aren't dogs. They're precipitates of night and fog, the murk the graphics cannot come through.[6]

What's more striking is that all killers, animal or human, are male. This may be literally true. But the truth, if that's what it is, has been sublimated into myth. In turn the myth reacts upon certain facts, distorting them, then 'naturalizing' the distortion. The resulting vision, along with its implied explanation of events, is just not credible. In *Suicide* the great ideological leap consists not in the assumption that only males are killers, but that with a few questionable exceptions, only killers have penises. Male victims do not; their crotches are obscured. The myth demands this, because within it penises are interchangeable with weapons. Victims cannot have them. The insistent pictorial implication is that carnage issues from night, fog, and male genitalia. Oppression is envisioned as subpolitical, subrational, not socially managed. The suggestion of biological politics is disturbing, in itself and in that it mystifies the terms of South African oppression. The sexual mythification is so compelling that whipping, to give just one example, is illustrated by a man using a whip (a *sjambok*) as a penetrator on a fallen woman—he holds the whip-butt at his crotch, arcing the tip down into her groin area—willfully denying the way a whip *in fact* afflicts and terrifies. There are many such instances of anatomical and/ or instrumental penises signaling aggression and brutishness.[7]

The male/beast mythification culminates in an apocalyptic image of bestiality: a $-branded dog, under the sign of WAR, stretches over dismembered victims as it (he) fucks yet another victim clinging to its underside. We can't say the victim is being screwed—that is too idiomatically blanched a word to convey what is depicted. Nor can the enormous image be read as a metaphor for the specific oppression with which the South African ruling class, male and female, brutalizes the black underclass. Penis itself is the criminal instrument. Fucking is what the beast, and only the beast, does. The one positive sexual image does not involve black people; it appears, oddly, on the 'tsotsis' page: an anomalous cameo of one white woman feeling up another.[8] It's as though penis oppression were the latent subject of the graphics, and South Africa a medium for incorporating it. None of this is acknowledged by the text. The graphics are left competing with their subjects, the oppressed people of southern Africa, for the power to designate the terms of those subjects' oppression.

6

A side comment on dogs and text…The text of *Suicide* goes beyond the graphics in that it does project a solution. But the solution is magical, without instrumentation or agency to effect it. It solves nothing. To quote "the dogs will be killed," and to leave it at that, is to do less than the paintings on cave walls did. In its wishfulness the text does not think to ask how or by whom those dogs will be killed. The crucial question has still to be addressed.

7

There is a further mystification. Time and again the graphics resort to traditional Christian mythology. In the torture of Biko we have a demonic yet classical Pietà. On the Soweto 1976 page, a foot-of-the-Cross tableau with the victim's arms outstretched and the feet still overlapped; elsewhere, one crucified with his own blood; and an enigmatic red-haired figure with stigmata. Also the Shroud of Turin or the Veil of Veronica: a woman standing at the head of an open casket, holding a cloth on which the features of the half-effaced corpse are imprinted. The religious symbology and allusions are meant to illuminate, amplify and elevate the suffering of the victims. They only mythify that suffering. They mask it, make it opaque, consigning it to the dead end of metaphysical awe.

Marx in *The 18th Brumaire* observes that those who struggle through revolutionary crises "anxiously conjure up the spirits of the past to their service and borrow from them names, battle cries and costumes in order to present the new scene of world history in [a] time-honored disguise and [a] borrowed language. Thus Luther donned the mask of the Apostle Paul, the Revolution of 1789 to 1814 draped itself alternately as the Roman republic and the Roman empire…" The mythification of Biko, Aggett and others as crucified Christs accommodates their deaths only by burying their lives. The meaning of those lives is suppressed.

It's little different with them than with Guevara, say, who is routinely deprived of specific historicity by being shut up in a prettified Christ mold. Whatever these people may be, and for all their considerable differences, they are not saviors descended on those who could not save themselves. They're distinct manifestations of those who must liberate their own collective self. As exemplary expressions of the struggle of oppressed people, Biko and Aggett are fulfilled in the realization of that struggle, not in being iconized.[9] Yet realized how? This is not a political question alone, but an aesthetic one. In the work quoted above, Marx adds that "the social revolution of the nineteenth century cannot draw its poetry from the past, but only from the future. It cannot begin with itself before it has stripped off all superstition in regard to the past. Earlier revolutions required recollections of past world history in order to drug themselves concerning their own content. In order to arrive at its own content, the revolution of the nineteenth century must let the dead bury their dead. There the phrase went beyond the content; here the content goes beyond the phrase." This is not the nineteenth century. In certain respects, it's tempting to add, this is not *yet* the nineteenth century. And *Suicide* is not a work of social revolution. Even so, Biko and Aggett deserve a language, a graphics, that rises to their occasion.

The question is not how to do aesthetic justice to the struggle for social justice, a concern beyond this book, but how to articulate social indignation. This is a problem rarely taken on by artists in this country, and it's to the immense credit of Coe and Metz that they have attempted it. That *Suicide* pulls up short, that it misperceives, is not the most significant thing about it. What is, is that it declines to ironize, and that it refuses to withdraw behind a wall of caution. In fact we *need* such failures so we may learn better what to do and how to do it. For cultural workers, the technical struggle is for a language or imagery that will not fall all over itself, failing its own purpose. For that reason alone this is a work to attend to. Obviously the sexual and religious mythifying are not adequate to contend with the historical reality of apartheid. Not adequate *aesthetically*. But then, even aesthetic solutions come through engagement in concrete struggle, not through speculation or dehistoricized analogy, nor through the uncritical adoption of images conditioned by other specific struggles. There *is* sexual oppression, and it is pervasive, but it is not the linchpin of apartheid.

8

The conceptual difficulties facing the producers of this book are extraordinary. The irony of official South African 'suicide' is so transparent, so instantaneously exhaustible, that it almost defies elaboration. South African 'suicide' takes the web of language, which is after all a social understanding, and pulls the string out.[10] Worse, because it is backed by state power, *that* 'suicide' reconstitutes *our* word 'suicide.' What had been a consensus meaning, as it appears in current dictionaries, must accommodate this quite differently elaborated meaning. (By the same token, given that 'the free world' means, as we all recognize it means, South Africa, Turkey, Chile, El Salvador, South Korea, Honduras and the like, it's clear that the word 'free' has been effectively reconstituted, and that present dictionary definitions hide as much as they reveal about the socially empowered and enacted meaning of that word.)

We had understood suicide to be a prerogative of individuals. Even the etymology of 'suicide' identifies it as a self-reflexive act. But now a distinct (less mediated) social dimension has been impressed upon the word. At one level, our recognition of South African 'suicide' as nothing but plain murder reminds us that language, visual language included, is not made of words or markings alone. Yet at another level we are faced with the realization that the 'suicide' which is 'murder' is, politically, a suicide of immense and complex proportion. Apartheid itself, in terms not only of species but of polity, is social suicide. So what then are we left with? What does 'suicide' mean? It means *what it is socially empowered to mean*. Meanings of words are historically enacted and validated through their social currency. Meanings are not ahistorically given, as guardians-of-the-language dictionary-makers have sometimes mistakenly assumed. When murder is suicide—not said to be, but historically enforced to the point that it *is* suicide—how are we to respond to this imposition, this contemptuous reconstitution of our language? Of what, rather, we had thought was our language. What is an appropriate and effective *aesthetic* response?

Suicide freeze-frames the nightmare of despair. A different tack is taken by the German poet Erich Fried in his poem on the 'suicide' of Ulrike Meinhof, a journalist and writer who was a founding member of the Red Army Faction, a group depoliticized (criminalized) by West German authorities and media as the "Baader-Meinhof Gang." In 1976 she was found dead in her high-security cell in Stammheim prison. Meinhof wasn't the only prisoner 'suicided' there. Nonetheless Fried writes particularly of her.

1
She was driven to
political madness
by the
politically normal
and their norms

2
If she could still write
she herself would have to write
the definitive report
on her death

and review
the evidence for suicide
and weigh it
bit by bit

and say
who it was
that committed
this suicide

However Meinhof's politics are characterized, as vanguard or adventurist or worse, they had to have been lonely. Fried airs the desolated irony of her politics, and the politics of the "politically normal," and the death in which they coincide. His response may be nominally adequate at best, but it is a beginning. It clears ground—facing, taking the measure of, a reality that holds *all* language in contempt. What Fried does not do is pursue this to where the question is not merely one of judgment or of language, but of response and technique. Of what to do, and how to do it. Of how to get beyond political and aesthetic incapacitation.

9

Cultural workers in particular are reminded, pointedly, that historical reality keeps talking back. What isn't in *Suicide* turns up in the news. What was suppressed bursts into view. An item in the *New York Times* (7 Sept. 1984) describes how the South African Ministers of Defence, Education, and Internal Affairs toured the scenes of recent protest violence "in a bus encased in iron grilles and escorted by armored trucks." Then, near Sebokeng, "as they crested a low rise, with escort helicopters above, their convoy came to an abrupt halt because hundreds of people, about 500 yards down the rock-littered highway in front of them, seemed to have formed a human barricade across their route, a presence of vague menace, lighted by a low sun. Without investigating further, the ministers withdrew." This vignette, telling in itself, might have been accommodated within the visual tonalities of this book. Yet had it been available, such an account would still have been ideologically inadmissible within *Suicide*. The book would not be what it is, it would have to reconstitute itself, if the graphics were to acknowledge a *humanizing show of power*, admitting to a violence that *negates* brutalization.

Finally, we don't have to be scared or demoralized, nor confirmed in our rectitude. A genuine, effective humanity would instruct us not only in the fear but also in the anger, resilience and determination of those people. Would expand on what constitutes their, our, humanity. Would encourage. There is no inherent virtue in being victimized. Stronger than the oversized sheets of red-rimmed and creased murkiness is the "Women's Freedom Song," apparently the only southern African art to come through these opaque pages.

> Now you have touched
> the woman
> you have struck

a rock,
you have dislodged
a boulder,
you will be crushed...

Now that is strong, politically and aesthetically. It is coherent, efficient, eloquent, tactically alert and subtle, from *touched* to *crushed*.[11] It does what a considered, serious art, gotten beyond posturing, can do. And it defines freedom positively: as movement, as assurance, as powerful overcoming.

10

Some years ago Hannah Arendt's book on the trial of Adolf Eichmann caused a controversy. Taking issue with the Israeli prosecutor, who made Eichmann a bigger-than-life monster, she insisted on the "banality" of that Nazi bureaucrat who expedited mass murder. Arendt may have pushed the point— "banality" is an attitudinizing, condescending category— making a seemingly paradoxical assessment a provocative one. Yet she could not have been more serious. By mythifying oppression we block understanding and put ourselves at a loss in contending with it. Monstrous social policies and conditions are not biologically or metaphysically ordained. The 'beasts' are people become agents, *functionaries*, of an exploitive, dehumanizing, murderous system.[12] They are to be judged and responded to not according to what they supposedly 'are,' but with regard to what they do. There's nothing mysterious about this, nor about what is necessary (as distinct from what is sufficient, a more problematical matter) to achieve a solution. The system of exploitation must be destroyed. It's not enough to decry it. It deforms people and their production, including cultural production. To support effective resistance to that system may be the most humane, aesthetically fulfilling course an artist *as* artist can take. The alternatives, most of which are based on immobilizing fantasies of aesthetic autonomy, hardly bear thinking on.

1   See *The Sun Will Rise: Statements from the Dock by Southern African Political Prisoners*, Mary Benson, ed. (London: International Defense & Aid Fund, 1981). Also Indres Naidoo's *Robben Island* (New York: Vintage, 1983), an account of his ten years as a prisoner. What comes through is a sense of prisoners living not a nightmare but a struggle. They are also witty. Significantly there is no place for such people, nor their outlook, in *Suicide*.

2   A commonplace of liberal ideology. H. Bruce Franklin, in *Prison Literature in America* (Westport, Conn.: Lawrence Hill & Co., 1978), summarizes and quotes academic responses to Frederick Douglass's claim that he had freed *and humanized* himself through repelling "by force the bloody arm of slavery." Taking issue with Douglass's evaluation of his own actions, one critic finds "irony in the situation in which Douglass must reduce his conflict with the slaveholders to a question of brute strength and physical violence in order to assert his 'manhood.'" (Though Douglass does use the word 'man'—e.g., "you have seen how a man was made a slave; you shall see how a slave was made a man"—it's clear that he refers to his humanity, his status as a human being. The critic distorts and trivializes Douglass's concern, displacing it with his own sexual, even sexist, one.) The critic goes on to state the values that Douglass *ought* to have had, explaining that Douglass's "most splendid assertion of his manhood was...his triumph over language and his own rage." Yet as Douglass demonstrates, such 'triumph' only aggravates his misery and drives him deeper into brutishness. It is indeed necessary for him to master reading and writing, but it is not sufficient. His rage enables his liberation not through being conquered or suppressed, but by virtue of its being *informed*. As Franklin sums it up, "Unlike those who think a person becomes a 'brute' when he or she fights back against oppression, Douglass has shown us that the brutes on the farm are

those who remain sheepish; those who can learn how to resist and defeat slavery are truly human beings."

3   Denial is a function of idealist (undialectical, ahistorical) moralizing. In a comment on reactive sentimentalism, Marx observes that "any developmenting...can be represented as a series of different stages of development that are connected in such a way that one forms the *negation* of the other. If...a people develops from absolute monarchy to constitutional monarchy, it *negates* its former political being. In no sphere can one undergo a development without negating one's previous mode of existence. *Negating* translated into a language of morality means: *denying.*

      "Denying! With this catchword the Philistine as critic can condemn any development without understanding it; he can solemnly set up his undevelopable undevelopment beside it as moral immaculateness..." From "Moralizing Criticism and Critical Morality." From this perspective, Grosz is as much Philistine as his philistines.

4   Despite domestication, dogs continue to have a darker range of associations. E.g., Auden's "In the nightmare of the dark / All the dogs of Europe bark, / And the living nations wait / Each sequestered in its hate..." ("In Memory of W. B. Yeats"). Or the ominous nursery rhyme: "Hark, hark / The dogs do bark, / The beggars are coming to town; / Some in rags, / And some in jags, / And one in a velvet gown."

      Of course these are aural disturbances, warnings rather than direct threats. They pre-date the systematizing of that menace, the purposeful politicizing of it, which occurs with the development and maintenance of attack dogs as part of the state's police apparatus. It's the latter that preoccupies *Suicide.*

5   The 'beastifying' might have been intended to reveal the oppressors as prehuman: frozen back down on the evolutionary scale. But in this book there is no implied concept of an evolutionary mechanism or process. The beast faces are simple mythifications.

6   It's instructive to compare these with Heartfield's most memorable 'dog': the hyena in his corpse-strewn photomontage *War and Corpses: The Last Hope of the Rich.* That work has an analytical power that frees it from the ever-ever land of nightmare, putting it where it belongs: in the world we make our living in. The hyena's top hat, which was not then a dead metaphor but an accoutrement of the big bourgeoisie and its officials, bears an appropriate class identification. The motto on the Great War (World War I) flying medal draped about the scavenger's thick neck has been altered. Where that motto once read "for merit," it now says "for profit." In this way Heartfield calls attention to the link between bourgeois 'honor' and carnage. But the

main point is that this photomontage does not merely reinforce the horror, does not milk helpless emotion. It gives us something to think *and act* on. The image focuses not only on the sensationalism, the brutalizing consequence, but on what it's a consequence *of.*

In certain respects a corollary to the Heartfield photomontage might be *Suicide*'s spread on the Sharpeville massacre. The dominant figure, amidst corpses and one cowering victim, is a policeman whose SA insignia evokes SS lightning bolts. He has the face of a boar (a pun on Boer?) or a crocodile with razory teeth. The other killers are a second uniformed cop, who has a baboon face, a man in a bowler pointing a rifle at the groin area of a fallen, robed female figure, and a dog over a corpse. But these figures are absorbed into the sexual mythicizing that confronts the viewer like a wall, marking the end of action and of thought.

7   See pages 3, 6, 8-9,12,18, 20, 24-25, 29, 32-33, 35, 38-39, 40. One possible exception is the red-haired deity on page 15. The other seeming exception, though it's anything but, is the strung-out black wino on page 37, an image uglier than was doubtless intended. In another context the drunken man might have been pathetic. But in a book whose graphics demonize male genitalia—in effect making the penis the mark of the beast—the unusual tumescence showing through the man's trousers, its presence crudely reinforced by the bottle neck he holds at crotch level, marks him as *beastly*. This is not because we insist on that association, but because the graphics routinely do. The graphics have encoded male genitalia as instruments or as emblems of barbarism and even, it sometimes seems, of evil.

8   Apart from a Reagan head and a white military rapist, the only other whited 'white' is one, in miniature, leading a bloodied black man, though to what end is not clear. The inside front cover also has ironic photos of white women in bikinis enjoying a South African vacation. But whites in their savaging capacity are usually depicted as obscure beasts without specific racial characteristics.

9   The manipulation of religious imagery should not be confused with the realization of a religious medium. For instance, condemned prisoners singing hymns—including, I've heard, Blake's *Jerusalem*, which in that context is a powerful indictment of the actual land in which those prisoners have lived and are to die. The hymns are, as well, enacted expressions of solidarity. In *A Window on Soweto* (London: International Defence & Aid Fund, 1977), Joyce Sikakane reports how "when condemned prisoners were going to be hanged, then we could hear singing coming from the men's section in the early hours of the morning, long, never-ending hymns. This meant the men knew a hanging was about to take place."

10 This happens so often it's hardly noticed. In Chile, when General Pinochet was confronted with evidence of torture, he didn't deny that evidence. He simply responded that the prisoners practiced self-torture to gain sympathy and support. And recently, in a CBS newscast noting the deaths of two U.S. mercenaries involved in a *contra* bombing raid in Nicaragua, a raid that killed a cook and three girls picking fruit, the report was headlined "Mission of Mercy," implying that that's what the mercenaries had been up to. Dan Rather neglected, however, to reveal how they had exercised that mercy, and on whom.

11 In *Suicide* the power and subtlety are obscured because of the insensitive way the lines are broken: "Now you have / touched the / woman / you have struck / a rock, you / have dislodged / a boulder / you will be / crushed."

12 "The trouble with Eichmann was precisely that so many were like him, and that the many were neither perverted nor sadistic, that they were, and still are, terribly and terrifyingly normal. From the viewpoint of our legal institutions and of our moral standards of judgment, this normality was much more terrifying than all the atrocities put together…" This from Arendt's *Eichmann in Jerusalem* (New York: Viking, 1963). As she notes also, the worst was that Eichmann had not, as many claimed, "chosen to put himself outside all organized communities" so as to become "the enemy of all alike." On the contrary, one of the fundamental problems posed by crimes such as his was that "they were, and could only be, committed under a criminal *law* and by a criminal *state.*"

POETIC FREEDOM AND 'CUBA'

in Princeton, New Jersey

This is not about poetry or freedom in Cuba. It's not about Cuba at all. This concerns *assumptions* about artistic freedom—assumptions of the sort provoked by 'Cuba,' a symbol based on a country that professes socialism. 'Cuba,' then, is a term of convenience, one which figures as well in the piece that has provoked these comments: a poetry-and-freedom manifesto by Heberto Padilla and other Cuban exile writers publishing out of Princeton, New Jersey.

That said, the fact remains that neither the spectre of 'Cuba' nor the endowed presence of Princeton is decisive here. The crucial term is "freedom." Like Humpty Dumpty's "glory," freedom means whatever it is made to mean. (For Humpty, as for his world, "glory" is "a nice knock-down argument.") Once freedom has been defined, other values and categories follow from it. Where a person's 'freedom' is, there will his or her 'Cuba' or Princeton be.

1   bourgeois freedom

However bourgeois freedom may be fantasized, it presumes that each person is self-constituted as an individual subject. An indivisible subject that is socially buffeted, perhaps, but not socially constituted. The fantasy is not without consequence. It demands that freedom be conceived as a property rather than a quality. As a property, 'freedom' is congealed, commodified, divided among individuals. Freedom becomes at once scarce and overabundant, radically uneven in its two-faced development. The more such freedom one person or group has, the less others have. Metonymically, property-constituted freedom is implicated with colonialism and imperialism, whose singular *MORE!* is

118

accountable for multitudes of *less*. This according to the dictates of its own logic.[1]

"The liberty of the few is, in bourgeois social relations, built on the unfreedom of the many," as Christopher Caudwell put it. "Though anarchy, according to bourgeois theory, is complete liberty, in practice the bourgeois speedily sees that to live in the jungle is not to be free. Property is the basis of his mode of living...Thus the bourgeois contradicted his theory in practice from the start. The State took its distinctive modern form as the enforcement of bourgeois rights by coercion. Police, standing army and laws were all brought into being to protect the haves from the 'free' desires of the have-nots. Bourgeois liberty at once gave rise to bourgeois coercion, to prisons, armies, contracts, to all the ideology and education centered round the sanctity of private property, to all the bourgeois commandments."[2]

> I went to the Garden of Love
> And saw what I never had seen:
>
> A Chapel was built in the midst
> Where I used to play on the green
>
> And the gates of this Chapel were shut
> And "Thou shalt not" writ over the door...
>
> —William Blake, from
> "The Garden of Love"

Bourgeois 'freedom' is not simply built on unfreedom, as though a metaphysical unfreedom could exist on its own. Bourgeois 'freedom' produces unfreedom as surely as bourgeois 'wealth' expropriates wealth and well-being, so to produce the poverty it needs in order to exist. This is the 'freedom' the bourgeois associates with art, and would condition art on. It is the 'freedom' Padilla so righteously defends from his sanctuary in Princeton, New Jersey.

2   the case in point

'Freedom' and 'poetry' are not transcendent categories. They were not handed down from on high (though they are, or may be, projected from above), nor inscribed in genes. They are historically conditioned and are bound, however loosely or complexly, into social power. Each is as implicated in the web of social relations and values as we ourselves are. The power to call 'poetry' poetry, or to enforce a literary canon by means of publishing corporations and hegemonic academic institutions—the power to make an ideological, historically specific designation seem natural and therefore universal— is one with the power, say, to pass off 'human rights' as human rights.[3] It is the power to present a class-serving projection as a class-transcendent fact or revelation. So too the category 'freedom,' which the bourgeoisie conceives, naturally, in its own image.

In *Linden Lane Magazine,* a tabloid published in Princeton by Padilla, the editorial reads:

> ...we dedicate these pages to liberty. There is no better definition of liberty than the fact that a group of writers are able to get together—without any need to consult political police—in order to carry out the initiative of publishing an artistic and literary magazine. In the face of other definitions, this is the one that pleases us the most: Whoever tells us that the pursuit of social justice or the eradication of poverty must of necessity postpone or suppress the exercise of freedom shall and should be our enemy.[4]

Perhaps there is no need for U.S. poets *as* poets to consult the political police. Most such poets police themselves well enough. No one goes to them for news, as for instance we might go to a Dalton or a Różewicz for news, not even news of a psychological order. Those poets know what they are not supposed to touch on. They overlook or avoid what they are supposed to…a maneuver made 'natural' by the fact that poetry, as defined in bourgeois cultural relations and mythology, may be produced from certain subject-positions but not from others. Poetry may be produced by the transcendental subject who ruminates and 'feels,' but not by the socialized subject who thinks and acts. As defined in bourgeois terms, it most certainly may not be produced by the incompletely victimized victim who attacks the systemic bases of bourgeois power. That *cannot* be 'poetry.' So Padilla's notion of police, as we see, is simplistic. Communication and distribution systems, along with academic institutions, themselves serve policing functions, a job for which they are more than adequate. Had Padilla himself expressed or enacted politics of a different sort, he would hardly have been welcomed at Princeton or by his U.S. publisher. His literary freedom would have been declared 'political,' and support withdrawn. He may not be aware of this, but then he has no need to be, as his program dovetails so nicely into the ideological landscaping of Linden Lane.[5]

Still, the manifesto is an astonishing document. Padilla and his associates defend freedom of speech, which should be defended, but do so in terms effectively denying that freedom. Their 'freedom of speech,' actually of literary speech, is made to self-destruct. What does it mean, historically, to define liberty as the freedom to publish a literary magazine, and to grant that 'freedom' militant, unconditional precedence over freedom from poverty or social injustice? Although a Turkish or Haitian peasant might find Padilla's 'freedom' something of a sick joke—and wonder at his self-absorption—we may nonetheless concede that his outlook and experience have led him in all innocence to this pass, which is also an impasse.

In Cuba he was prevented from publishing whatever he

wished to publish. It's difficult to understand why. Padilla's poems, judging from those published in this country, amble about in a defiant, ineffectual solitude.

> Las Derechas me alaban
>   (ya me difamarán)
> Las Izquierdas me han hecho célebre
>   (¿no han empezado a alimentar sus dudas?)
> Pero de todas formas
> advierto que vivo entre las calles.
> Voy sin gafas ahumadas.
> Y no llevo bombas de tiempo en los bolsillos
> ni una oreja peluda—de oso.
> Ábranme paso ya
> sin saludarme, por favor.
> Sin hablarme.
> Échense a un lado si me ven.
>
>   —"Autorretrato del otro"

> The Right praises me
>   (in no time they will defame me)
> The Left has given me a name
>   (have they not begun to have doubts?)
> But at any rate I warn you
> I'm alive in the streets.
> I don't wear dark glasses.
> And I don't carry time bombs in my pockets
> or a hairy ear—a bear's.
> Give me room, now.
> Don't greet me, I beg you.
> Don't even speak to me.
> If you see me, keep to one side.
>
>   —"Self-portrait of the other" [6]

Which is as strong as it gets. He takes a firm stand between the CIA or NSC (dark glasses, time bombs) and the KGB (a bear's hairy ear), before pretending to shun the reader he pretends to address…coyly inviting attention by protesting too much against it. This might have been an act of heroic self-abnegation, a way of (acting out) protecting the nondescript reader from guilt by association, except that four times in succession he makes the same self-conscious gesture. At best he melodramatizes his own real plight. The gesture is disingenuous—concerned above all, regardless of its truthful or factual basis, with being self-serving. That the Cuban government should feel threatened by this standard Romantic gesture, the individuating pose of a lonely ego, does not say much for that government—unless of course there were, as there seem not to have been, substantive reasons for its response.[7] As perceived by the Cuban government, and possibly by Padilla himself, there was a conflict between its intention to meet the needs of the neediest, or of the majority, and Padilla's own desires and values. Padilla's manifesto does not question the genuineness of the government's intention, whatever he himself may think. His philosophically far-reaching claim is that the intention, genuine or not, is based on an unacceptable hierarchy of values. The conflict between Padilla and the government had come to a head when he was awarded Cuba's prestigious Writer's Union Poetry Prize. At the time he was a correspondent for Prensa Latina, the Cuban press agency. He was recalled home, placed under house arrest, and later exiled. Reportedly he was imprisoned for 38 days.

Padilla is sincere. He has suffered for his beliefs, which in metaphysical isolation are unexceptionable (provided we subscribe to bourgeois values, fetishizing the transcendental subject). Yet as we know, abstract beliefs may be bought and sold. Even when concretized, beliefs are not and never have been validated by suffering alone no matter how terrible. (To take a notorious case: that Solzhenitsyn suffered for his beliefs in a labor camp, and suffered at length, does not make those beliefs any less antidemocratic, xenophobic or racist.) Beliefs are constituted in and through their history: they are what, in life, they come to. Padilla's perspective is so classbound— poverty or earning a livelihood are not telling concerns within that perspective—that he's unable to entertain the obvious. Namely, that the non-pursuit of social justice and the perpetuation of poverty must *of themselves necessarily* "postpone or suppress the exercise of freedom." Poverty and social injustice, the denial of literacy and education, the direct and indirect deprivation of life's basic possibilities and, sometimes, of life itself, also take away the freedom to publish a literary magazine. They take away the freedom *to think of* publishing a literary magazine—and take that freedom away on a scale, to a depth, inconceivable in Padilla's terms. The freedom obliterated by poverty and social injustice is not Padilla's freedom to publish—a 'freedom' not only compatible with social injustice and poverty, but also under the present capitalist system positively requiring it—but the freedom of most of the world's people to do so, or even to dream of doing so.

A class-serving value has been advertised as a transcendent 'human' value. That the advertisement is sincere does not make it less fraudulent. And that Padilla has become the function of a situation does not make him any less the functionary of an ideology. Having come up against a painful dilemma, he has reacted blindly. The most to be said is that his manifesto does have a Thermopylaean air about it: he and his allies are holding the narrow pass of high bourgeois culture against the bumbling onslaughts of a striving for social justice.

This is not his problem but ours. Padilla does no more than defend his class and its values, even though it's a class for whom poetry, meaning its own poetry, is little more than an emblem or 'point of honor.' We, though, have to get beyond the terms of his culturally impoverished class: to achieve, we hope, conditions whereby 'poetry' may aspire to become poetry. Become, that is, a practice coextensive with the entire range of social life. A *practice*, because engaged in the struggle to realize humanity—not, as in the *Linden Lane* proclamation, an ideological function that must, to sustain itself, cannibalize the greater part of human life and lives.

Any 'poetry' or 'freedom' that necessarily contravenes the full human realization of *all* is, as Padilla reveals, a nasty little business.

3   that other manifesto

Caudwell noted that "bourgeois freedom is almost as imprisoning to its enjoyers as the worker's unfreedom." So it is. That is why, as we read the deliberately phrased anticipation of the *Communist Manifesto,* that "in place of the old bourgeois society, with its classes and class antagonisms, we shall have an association, in which the free development of each is the condition for the free development of all," we realize that nothing could be further from the barbarism of *Linden Lane* 'freedom.' Ultimately, the privileged space of Princeton, reserved for the precious few, is extracted from the Miami detention camps, the Krome Avenues set aside for the incarceration of Haitian boat people, for the internment of their darker skins and their poverty. Their unfreedom—the very basis of Padilla's freedom, its *sine qua non*—is what makes that freedom so wretched. That is also why his self-immersed poetry may not dwell upon its premises, which is to say, the sorry conditions upon which that poetry rests.

1   "For those who see history as a competition, Latin America's backwardness and poverty are merely the result of its failure. We lost; others won. But the winners happen to have won thanks to our losing: the history of Latin America's underdevelopment is...an integral part of the history of world capitalism's development. *Our defeat was always implicit in the victory of others; our wealth has always generated our poverty by nourishing the prosperity of others—the empires and their native overseers. In the colonial and neocolonial alchemy, gold changes into scrap metal and food into poison.*" Eduardo Galeano, *Open Veins of Latin America* (New York: Monthly Review Press, 1973), 12-13.

2   Christopher Caudwell, *Liberty: A Study in Bourgeois Illusion* (New York: Oriole Editions, n.d.). Published originally in *Studies in a Dying Culture*, 1938.

3   That the American chapter of P.E.N. has a "Freedom to Write" committee hints at its class-conditioned perspective. P.E.N. is often progressive, but within bourgeois-dictated terms. In the U.S., where nearly a third of the population is functionally illiterate, that organization has not made literacy a priority. Yet the freedom to be literate, especially as no one is *naturally* illiterate, would seem, in the absence of class bias, cause for overriding concern.

For an early statement as to how and why class values are sublimated into 'natural' or 'universal' ones, see Marx and Engels: "The class which has the means of material production at its disposal, has control at the same time over the means of mental production, so that thereby...the ideas of those who lack the means of mental production are subject to it. The ruling ideas are nothing more than the ideal expression of the dominant material relationships, the dominant material relationships grasped as ideas...The individuals composing the ruling class possess among other things consciousness, and therefore think. Insofar...as they rule as a class and determine the extent and compass of an epoch, it is self-evident that they do this in its whole range, hence among other things rule also as thinkers, as producers of ideas, and regulate the production and distribution of the ideas of the epoch...[Their] ideas...take on the form of universality. For each new class which puts itself in the place of the one ruling before it, is compelled, merely in order to carry through its aim, to represent its interest as the common interest of all the members of society...it has to give its ideas the form of universality, and represent them as the only rational, universally valid ones..." *The German Ideology* (New York: International Publishers, 1970), 64-66.

4   *Linden Lane Magazine,* Jan.-March 1982, 32. Padilla and associates observe that "Linden Lane is the name of the Princeton street where our magazine is edited. This name was chosen by the founders of this town, a town historically connected to the American struggle for

liberty and democracy, and always has been a refuge for those writers and artists persecuted by the tyrannies of our age. It is not an industrial center; rather it is a quiet yet active workshop, where intelligence is allowed its own freedom." Poor Trenton, poor Newark, poor Bayonne! Brute industrial centers...what are they to do without Padilla, without the intelligence that flourishes, oh so freely, in Princeton?

5   We may be fairly certain that, as Padilla signed this group document, he must have written it. At the 48th International P.E.N. Congress, when "asked whether he would sign a petition critical of United States policy toward Nicaragua, Mr. Padilla [refusing] replied, 'I sign only what I write.'" *New York Times*, Jan. 28,1986.

6   Heberto Padilla, *Legacies: Selected Poems* (New York: Farrar Straus Giroux, 1982), 152-55. Translated by Alastair Reid and Andrew Hurley.

7   The case of Armando Valladares comes to mind. Valladares was the 'prison-crippled poet' who, it turned out, had been a police agent for Batista, the former dictator. According to Saul Landau: "Valladares appears to have included in his book every prison horror story known as if they happened to him. The Cuban government did demonstrate that Valladares simulated paralysis while he was in prison. Aside from a surreptitious video tape that shows Valladares leaping from his wheelchair in the hospital bathroom and doing exercises, the leading Cuban orthopaedic specialist and a team of experts from the Medical School examined him and found no organic cause for paralysis and concluded that he was faking. When Valladares was freed, TV news cameras showed him walking normally and even running as he disembarked from the airplane." Saul Landau, "Asking the Right Questions about Cuba," *Race & Class* 29:2 (1987), 68.

LINE BREAK

1   conceiving technique

Toward the end, one of the ends, of *A Theory of Literary Production,* Pierre Macherey makes two observations that may apply to the question of lineation, of line breaks as poetic devices. The first is that "the activity of the writer is not solely or directly governed by the laws of stylistics, defined in themselves: on the contrary, it is his activity that determines those laws. The writer is not someone who 'practices stylistics,' consciously or unconsciously...He encounters certain specific problems, which he solves as he writes, and these problems, and the solutions which actually constitute them, are never simple, unlike those of stylistics. The writer is constantly obliged to solve several problems at once, at different levels, and each choice affects all the others..."[1]

Macherey makes short work of "stylistics"—the pastime of those who, unconcerned that forms or conventions constitute and enact social content, hold to 'the rules of the game' as though that's all poetry were. To administer stylistics is to follow a historically articulated prescription, mindless of its history, so as to come up with something that looks and sounds like what 'poetry' is *supposed* to look and sound like. Stylistics, then, is not what this paper is about. For now, what's worth remarking is the apparent paradox that the exercise of stylistics, the foregrounding of what passes for technique, nonetheless comes through as technically impoverished. Conceiving technique as a thing-in-itself, those who play the stylistics game set out to do what they know how to do rather than what they have to do. They use technical devices they have appropriated (whose superficies they have appropriated) instead of developing the technique that their problematic demands.[2] Yet a repertory of technical devices is no substitute for technique or technical capability.

Writers in their writing practices attempt to solve those problems they have set for themselves, but set in concert with their historical circumstances, social values, class outlook, jobs, and the innumerable opaque or transparent 'aesthetic' or 'extra-aesthetic' encouragements and discouragements visited on them. For writers as writers the strict intramural question will be whether their technical capabilities have risen to the occasions of those problems: problems that are multifaceted, complex, involving more than immaterial linguistic equations. Writers have also to question whether their techniques have become extensions of the problems they would resolve. They have constantly to gauge the extent to which technique may have degenerated into technical devices. After all, "writer" is not a metaphysical category. To write is to resist the inclination to slip into cruise control. To resist giving up, or giving over. *Writing is a struggle against stylistics.*

Yet writing, like any social practice, is beset by the gamut of social concerns and conditions, by giddiness, reward, fatigue, demoralization, complacency—the insidious pressures of systemic ideological inertia. The pressure is more intense when, under the individuating conditions of bourgeois cultural production, phases of this social practice occur in solitary. It is easy to lose bearings, to submit and dissolve. Macherey's caution that "the writer is constantly obliged to solve several problems at once, at different levels," and that "each choice affects all the others," should be watermarked into every poem and impressed on every critical essay. The simplest decisions about line breaks will ramify, affecting not only the structural economy of a poem but its social practice, the way it works *as* a poem.

For instance, we know that a line break will influence the way a word or syllable is attacked (in the sense that a musician attacks a note). But the difference between one possible line break and another determines more than whether a particular word is taken in stride or "happened upon." The difference affects not only the work's internal relations, how as an object it is constructed, but its social practice. When line breaks are shifted, posture and attitude change, along with assumptions about meaning, focus, expectations. The poem "plays" differently. As with dramatic productions, different enactments of a work constitute distinct social practices and understandings. The common work, the piece of writing that appears selfsame with what we share with others, may be no more significant than the historical production that realizes it. Our Shakespeare is not Ben Jonson's Shakespeare, nor Dryden's nor Coleridge's. Our "To His Coy Mistress" is hardly Marvell's—as, in regendered readings, the structural brutality of the piece wears through the considerable charm that had seemed to be 'the poem itself.' Reading, as production, is always contemporary. The poem is produced in the reader's enactment of a poetic text— which, no less than the production of a dramatic text, is played out here, now, where we live.

Even if we pretended to extricate a work from its social conditioning, its readers and enactments, we'd find the work is itself a web. In production a work becomes a text, a complex of discriminations and exclusions. (Though strictly speaking it's impossible to distinguish between a work and a text. No one knows what an unrealized, uninterpreted work would be like.) The work is work, however, and one is always in the middle of it. For that reason 'creation' is not creation but a kind of revision—re-vision conducted in light of much that is present and more that is not. We can't really pretend, then, to deal with a work-in-itself. The work as a text is conditioned, informed and confronted by layers of context. The situation whereby the writer faces "several problems at once" is yet more problematical in that there are no strictly internal alterations in a work. Textual gestures or alterations are assumptions about the way a work functions in the world, which is precisely its functioning as a poem. A piece of versified writing is not a poem but an aging, historically weathered and weathering occasion for one. The poem is what that writing, as text, is *doing*.

So poems are practices, not constructs. (Poems that are writings, that is, not those that are stylistics.) Consequently, translation is not translation of a thing but of a communication, of the charged air, between the work and its reader. Or, to rephrase the matter, the translation is *of* the reader inscribed in the text. In Andrei Voznesensky's "Striptease," set in a Manhattan strip joint, the subject imagines a stripper finishing her routine and coming over to the bar, clearly to do a number on *him*. But he's riding his own hobby horse, intent on discovering "America."[3]

> "Are you America?" I'll ask like an idiot;
> She'll sit down, tap her cigarette.
>
> "Are you kidding, kiddo?" she'll answer me.
> "Better make mine a double martini!"

She has a case on her hands. And the translation, by William Jay Smith, is quite effective. Yet another translator makes a more literal, i.e., 'work'-bound, version of the last line:

> "Get me an absinthe and martini."

Whereas Smith translated what transpires between text and reader, the other translator has considered the word-object itself the poem. What should have been translated is what the line *enacts*. If language is socially constituted (as a complex of historically situated meanings) then it may not be treated, simplistically, as a transparent or dehistoricized medium. An "absinthe and martini" is merely strange in American English. The Russian line is not 'merely strange' in Russian. It has *some* resonance—as, for North Americans of a certain class and generation, a double martini does. Smith's translation realizes the text as a poem, a social transaction, rather than fetishizing it as an ahistorical, desituated construct.

The usual critical questionings tend to rule out decisive considerations.[4] What is decisive is determined to be beneath consideration. Focusing on what they presuppose is important, critics often enough overlook what is significant. Or the significant may be suppressed for the simple reason that it is not respectable. Different formalities may render a work acceptable or unacceptable to different constituencies. At present, among publishers of bourgeois belles lettres, there seems to be an unspoken and doubtless unconscious consensus regarding line breaks. Imagine line breaks so casual, predictable, inert, so resourceless, that the poet might well have written in prose rather than verse ("verses" being lines and line-endings that the author assumes responsibility for, or that are presumed to be invested with purpose). Suppose the poet abandoned his or her nonfunctional line breaks. How might this be received by publishers who have a ritualized toleration for certain kinds of evasion, dislocation and silliness in 'poetry,' but who are unlikely to extend the exact same license to prose (which is indulged in other ways)? The de-versified writings might pass muster as prose poems, but only if there weren't too many of them, and only if they were unabashedly 'poetic,' meaning circuitous, hermetic, portentous, *reasonably* pointless. That possibility aside, our imaginary uncanonized poet could not opt for formal integrity, for writing over stylistics, even if he or she wanted to. The de-versified work would be unpublishable. (Printable maybe, but publishing is not printing. Publishing is advertising, plus access to national review and distribution systems.) Worse, our made-up poet would be less likely to think this awareness, to face his or her decision *as* a decision, than quietly to proceed on the basis of it. A 'technical' decision to break writing into lines will have been influenced by 'extrapoetic' concerns and circumstances. But then *all* poetic determinations are saturated with extrapoetic ones.

The layers of problems and problem-solving that inform the technical aspects of any work are immensely complex and subtle. And crude. They overrun the blinking and blindered ways, the mind-forged manacles, of self-styled literary criticisms. From the perspective of production, of producing poems and of reproducing them in reading, such criticisms seem naive. Not that we should be incapacitated by the enormity of it all, the complexity of the simplest technical issues. On the contrary, awareness of that complexity should temper and deepen our engagement with technical matters. It would be one thing if poetry were made of words alone, but it is not—no more than words themselves are.[5] Poems exist in and through the historically specific world they are formed in concert with, and that is why seemingly isolable technical questions are so complex. Questions of poetic technique are no less historically and socially conditioned than any other technical question.

Macherey observes that "one of the essential reasons for this complexity is that the work never 'arrives unaccompanied'; it is always determined by the existence of other works, which belong to different areas of production. There is no first book, independent and absolutely innocent: novelty and originality, in literature as in other fields, are always determined by relationships. Thus the book is always the site of an exchange: its autonomy and its coherence are bought at the price of that otherness, which can be, on occasion, an alteration" (p. 100). If for "the work" we substitute "meter"—or, regarding free verse, if we put "the handling of lines and line breaks" in place of the "the book"— we have some indication of the bare *intramural* complexity of technical questions. Meter never "arrives unaccompanied." And free-verse line breaks are always "the site of an exchange," not only with other free-verse line breaks but with those of prescribed verse as well. How a line breaks depends on how line breaks *have been* working—historically, in general in the present (not in poetry only, but in ads, in headlines, on labels, etc.), and in the specific, historically developing practice of the immediate producer of the lines, the writer.

2   technique 'takes place'

Even intramural questions are defined by permeable walls. They are not merely intramural after all, but are questions of *livings*. Contemporary poetic practice is contemporary social practice as well. A poetry or poem is the site of an exchange wherein the 'poetic' and the 'extrapoetic' lose the certainty of their abstracted categorical boundaries. It is also where synchronic and diachronic dimensions confer. A poem occurs in and across and through times. It weathers, seasons, maybe rots. Even within the historically shifting category of the 'poetic,' what is designated 'poetry' consists of many different poetries. It is never the same

One technique or technical device in one time and place is not the same at another, though to the metaphysical (undialectical) empiricist it may seem so. Take the prose poem. In France in the 1870s the prevailing verse was elaborate and restrictive. Rimbaud's prose poems (which were not the first, however) overwhelmed the prescribed poetic forms and manners of the time. They were writings in the place of stylistics. Yet their negation of the poetically dominant Parnassians' verse was only one aspect of the historical exchange. Exchange implies linkage, too. Rimbaud's prose poems, while distinguishing themselves from that other poetry, retain ties to it. They achieve definition by means of it. The Parnassians' practice conditions his, even as his comprehends theirs. His freewheeling 'unrealism' redeems their sometimes determined exoticism. Particulars may be argued, of course, but what's unquestionable is that his prose poems are a radically powerful social *intercourse*. They revolutionize not by denying the given 'poetic discourse' but by absorbing and negating it.[6]

Compared with those of Rimbaud and his predecessors, contemporary prose poems in English knock at an opened door. Appearances notwithstanding, they do not constitute the same technique as Rimbaud's do. They issue challenges, yet make no difference. Their conventional novelty is vitiated by an adherence to whatever passes for poetic diction, or to the 'poetically' sanctioned schematics and thematics that pass for substance. Like the social critic who bends over backward to confirm his or her patriotism (as in reformist red-baiting), or who otherwise feels compelled to seem respectable, most contemporary prose poems are more 'poetic' than poems in verse are. Consequently it's difficult to credit the attempt, by the author of a recent *New York Times* article, to distinguish between the old prose poetry which "seeks to constitute a single, unified experience," and a postmodernist kind which "dissolves experience, forcing the reader to establish a new experience out of language."[7] His examples show only that the two kinds of prose poem are, where it counts, *semblables* under the skin:

> "It's a white nest! White as the foam thrown up when the sea hits the rocks. Some light comes through it, we get the feeling of those cloudy transoms above Victorian doors, or of the manless hair of those intense nurses, gray and tangled after long nights in the Crimean wards. It is something made and then forgotten, like our own lives that we will entirely forget in the grave, when we are floating, nearing the shore where we will be reborn, ecstatic and black." [Robert Bly]

> "The lids of known things, dissolved behind the scenes. In place of remarks, read mournful silence. Each second the features repeat. These hills are the same ones they are. The past will contain the future. I found that I had put my shoes on backwards. I faced the other way. By the time he got there,

he had totally forgotten the way back. He was back home, out back. Audibly, it was centuries collapsing." [Bob Perelman]

There are differences between the two. The second piece hedges its prose by introducing a disguised line break (the uninstitutionalized comma between "things" and "dissolved," a device which passive-fies the predication). But what they share with other contemporary prose poems (John Ashbery's *Three Poems* is also approvingly cited in the article) is that they are all portent and "sensibility." Either is just another symptomatic literature.[8] What these have in common is the core of bourgeois ideology: the transcendental subject that in the Perelman piece is diffused (not dissolved) into a transcendent subjectivity. Perelman's shifting pronouns (the unspoken or signifier-less "you" of the second sentence, the "I" becoming yet possessing "he," the sentimentally generalized "it") no more challenge that subjectivity than do the metamorphosing pronouns of John Berryman's ritual end-man poetry. If anything they confirm it. It is this subjectivity, notwithstanding the veneer of deracinated patterns and motifs, that is the very medium of their coherence.

Prose poeming has largely degenerated into stylistics. The verse that might confront and galvanize it is more accommodating, uncertain, than that surrounding Rimbaud. Now the prosing of poetry would have to be carried further—certainly further than the above-cited pieces take it. To become a writing, the prose poem would have to go beyond the letter and into the ideological heartland of 'poetry.' The prose poem would have to negate poeticism, not redress it.

Finally there's no way to dehistoricize technique or limit it to the internal economy of a poem. Any technique *takes place*. It entails history, raises factors of education, class, cultural access, and so on. A technique is a relationship not simply to materials, though materials too are historically specific, but to an audience, a constituency. Imagine the audience preconditions for New Style verse of the T'ang Dynasty (its most impressive practitioner, Tu Fu). Not only did New Style prescribe a rigid syntactic parallelism, but in certain couplets the words of one line had simultaneously to match and to contrast, enter into pivotal relationship with, their counterparts in the other line. This is not to mention stipulations as to tone patterns and rhymes, nor a seemingly related historical tendency to become more densely allusive, privatized, until at the end of the geographical immensity and the personal insecurity there were, or there appear to be from here, a few unfathomable psychological chunks, like cavern fish grown strange in their lightless solitude (the poetry of Li Ho, 791-817). Yet the most obvious prerequisite for producing New Style verse, that the poet develop the skill to master its demanding specifications, may be the least significant. Any 'technique,' in the sense of stylistic, can be learned. If one person can manage it then countless others, given the opportunity and incentive, could do the same. Tu Fu could work the intricacies of New Style verse not because he learned how to do so—though he did, he had to—but because it was *socially* possible for him to do so. Socially possible for him *to be understood* to be doing so. He lived in a feudal world which required a stratum of highly educated clerks, civil servants (of a sort) and monks. Poetry writing was included in 'civil service' examinations. Education was extended in order to prepare managers and clerks to administer the military expansion, the coordination of civil affairs and the revenue-raising of the T'ang Dynasty. The needs of that dynasty produced, with its layer of literacy, a constituency for the complexities of New Style poetry. This is one of the more obvious ways in which New Style verse is historically implicated.[9]

3   stylistics

That poetic technique is historically situated means, technically, that the poet may do what he or she *can* do, but that what he or she can do is not determined by the poet alone. (Had Dickinson or Hopkins not been so well connected, their work might never have surfaced. Even with that, it did not exist until it *could* exist.) A minutely calibrated technique, if not socially realizable, becomes symptomatic of technical immaturity. Student writers frequently demonstrate this. Some years ago, though well past student days, I wrote a few poems in classical meters. One such poem, "Letter to David," was based on a Horatian adaptation of Sapphics. The poem attempted a stress version of the quantitative classical meter. It also echoed surface details, and tried to reconstitute the subtextual gesture and plangency, of an ode by Horace. The text began:

> Looking away from my study, I realized suddenly the winter's
>   gone, the shrunk pockets of snow
> drained down the hollows. I felt like a bankrupt. The high winds
>   have cost me
> $300 for heat—
> worse I might add, but the sordid details are hardly important
>   Accidents, diaries, these
> fossils dissolve into oil…

It is very nearly possible to date the poem by noting the price of its oil. But I might 'place' the poem in a more personal chronology by observing that, despite occasional counterpointing (e.g., shrunk, winds), the metrical norm is almost mechanically realized. The game-legged couplets may be hard to apprehend, especially if the longer of the lines has to be broken by the printer, but the choriambs ($-\cup\cup-$) anchoring the meter should be obvious. Or so I'd assumed, this being modeled on the famous ode, IV.7, *Diffugere nives,* the springtime backlash poem which in James Michie's translation begins:

> Snow's gone away; green grass comes back to the meadows and
>   green leaves
>   Back to the trees, as the earth
> Suffers her springtime change. Now last month's torrents,
>   diminished
>   Keep to their channels...

And continues:

> Yet be warned: each year gone round, each day-snatching hour says
>   "Limit your hopes: you must die."
> Frost gives way to the warm west winds, soon summer shall trample
>   Spring and be trodden in turn...[10]

Whatever Horace's meter accomplished, my transposed variation was at best a tour de force. The 'technique' was historically unrealizable. For the few who read contemporary poetry, the fewer who pick up metrical norms, and the handful who have a working familiarity with classical meters, this particular meter *still* does not effectively exist. What I had done, technically, was scrupulous and inept.

It's misleading to identify technique with received forms or dehistoricized devices, or to suggest that technique is primarily a function of individual skill. There is no technique independent of the life context through which it is realized. We may grasp this point by recalling how Marx and Engels summarized the materialist basis of their philosophical practice:

> ...we do not set out from what men say, imagine, conceive, nor from men as narrated, thought of, conceived, in order to arrive at men in the flesh...we set out from real, active men, and on the basis of their real life process we

demonstrate the development of the ideological reflexes and echoes of this life process.

Dehistoricized technical devices have, roughly, the status of those "ideological reflexes and echoes." They do not constitute technique; they are its residue. Like "ideological reflexes" they are (again to quote) "sublimates of [a] material life process which is empirically verifiable and bound to material premises...thus [*in themselves* they] retain no semblance of independence. They have no history, no development..."

Technical devices generated through particular practice have no capability apart from their material history, which is necessarily their social history. The attempt to revitalize gutted technical devices, or to revamp forms relative to forms, is an idealist, immaterial enterprise. That is why 'exclusively literary' attempts to revolutionize literature are accommodated and redeemed by prevailing ideology, the very ideology informing the 'traditional' literature apparently under attack. It's not for want of trying that such attempts fail, but because they pit symptoms against symptoms. They put one face in place of another, but at the head of the same moribund corpus. Unless they engage not only the issue but the *practice* of social power—engage it in specific historical terms, not as sublimated or compartmentalized into an imagined autonomous or semiautonomous artworld—they cannot be seminal.[11]

4   technical breakdown: recapitulation, disclaimer

We need a provisional, intramural history of poetic technique: one that may not explicitly engage the subtler extrapoetic conditions of poetic practice, but that will approach technique(s) historically, dialectically, rather than as a succession of devices or still lifes.[12] The absence of that history is disabling. Writers (not stylists, who are locked in synchronicity) do assume a technical history. Yet in our time there has been no serious attempt to theorize that history. When and where a history appears, it is as an encyclopedia of discrete fragments and arbitrary givens: a catalog of forms in space. The reasons why there is no such history are many and complex. For instance, even my generalizations about technique are based on the unarticulated technical history that informs, *and is a consequence of,* my own technical practice. There is no metahistorical source of illumination or (re)construction. I understand and reconstitute past technical practices by the light of my own practice (itself 'born' among untheorized absorptions), but that's all any writer does.[13] The point is, this discussion must take place in a primitive half-light. We haven't even begun to *desire* a shared understanding of what it is that we have been doing. Or why. There is no Darwin or Marx of poetry. Not even a Levi-Strauss. Poetic technique, like a de rigueur dead saint, is shrouded in more mist than the relations of (economic) production ever were.

There is no unpositioned, dehistoricized technique. No way to comprehend line breaks in themselves. It's not simply that these are socially specific practices, nor that there are different kinds of line breaks—as in the misconceived distinction between end-stopped and run-on lines—but that line breaks do not work the same way in ballad quatrains as in blank verse, nor in prescribed verse as in free verse.[14] Not all free-verse line breaks function in the same way either, though all are implicated together. It's easy to forget that free verse is every bit as traditional as prescribed verse. Free verse too has a lineage, a historically produced repertoire of conventions through which it works and to which it responds.

This means that what I'll have to say, in particular about line breaks, will be presumptuous as well as provisional. Still, customary ways of envisioning technique are idealist projections; they do not and cannot comprehend what actually goes on. They do not even try to. Stylistics is mistaken for writing, etiquette for decorum, fetishized method for technique. It has been assumed that technique may be reduced to the administration of dehistoricized forms. Yet it's not only reductive to generalize on apparent technical devices—when those devices are dehistoricized it's just as misleading to particularize them, that is, to slip into the mystifying disjointedness of empiricism.

5   free-verse line breaks as punctuation

Most contemporary verse in English is free verse. Its forms are not prescribed. One distinction between prescribed and free verse is that the prescribed form may have a mnemonic function that the other does not typically have. But then free verse, which on the whole is harder to memorize than prescribed verse, is conditioned by the circumstance that there is less and less *individual* need to "hold in mind." If literacy is not universal it has at least been generalized; and this is conditioned on, though not caused by, the widespread availability of paper, printing and the like. It's no accident that Walt Whitman, one of the earliest free versers and certainly the most assured, was a printer by trade, and was so before becoming a journalist or turning his hand to poetry. Free verse needs *and assumes* a memory that may be consigned to memory banks such as books and notebooks, not to mention their electronic extensions. With increasing dependence on such repositories, and with less individual need to remember, free verse becomes possible and even, perhaps, inevitable. Yet a significant contradiction emerges: the memory norm is raised *socially* (technological advancement not only allows but demands ever more highly detailed fact and data retention) while *individually,* due to increasing dependence on these storage systems, and apart from access to them, the norm is lowered. Individually we need not hold as much in mind.[15] Free verse, then, is predicated on social as well as technological developments, not the least being literacy, which as a mass phenomenon is a function of economy, of the demands of modern industrial and so-called postindustrial production.[16]

I cannot rehearse the historical conditioning of free verse, nor concoct a taxonomy of line breaks. Suffice it to say that those line breaks may be expressive. May reflect, refract or shift the angle and distance between the work and the reader. Or telescope meaning. Or render ideologically difficult meaning (more on this later) through the medium of an accessible or unresisted meaning. Line breaks define energy. They may let the air out, redistribute rhythm, shift the weight of a word, reset our relationship to it. They do this and more. But what's more significant is that the line break is the most volatile, productive punctuation in free verse. It is punctuation that has not been regulated or domesticated. It has not been theorized.

In certain respects free-verse line breaks function as some commas and semicolons do in the prose of Swift, or of Dr. Johnson—as gestures imparting edge, point, impact, shared *consciousness.* True, much of Johnson's prose punctuation is available to our own prose. He writes:

> The milder degrees of poverty are, sometimes,
> supported by hope; but the more severe often sink
> down in motionless despondence...

and we recognize that the (for us) optional commas around "sometimes" give the sentence voice, or the contours of voice. They make it telling. In so doing they bespeak not simply the author, but the author feeling (producing!) the presence of the reader. Without the reader, the inscribed one that is, those commas would not exist. They have no effect on the referent of the sentence, nor on the information it bears. Yet this our own punctuation can and does do. When Johnson writes his very next sentence, however, we realize what the necessary systematizing of prose punctuation has cost us. He could put it this way:

Life must be seen, before it can be known.

The comma is devastating. With it Johnson has taken our measure and written to the solar plexus. 'You thought you knew it all, did you? Well take *this*!' Or so the unpredictable comma seems to *impart* to us. Yet that comma is only doing what free-verse line breaks can do, and what systematized, categorizing punctuation no longer does. It is a chink in our shield of expectations, of what we think we know. It opens a crack in that control panel. It displaces the gerrymandered understandings we are constantly pressed to mistake for nature and truth itself.

Dr. Johnson's punctuation is an unembarrassed *practice*. Reading his prose, we have to keep alert. There's extraordinary give and take between the work and its reader, who is more necessary than ever for the realization of the work. In a sense Johnson's punctuation is fundamentally distinct from our own, because ours, unlike his, apportions, places and sorts in order *to* apportion, place and sort.[17] Ours is self-referential; its loyalty is to its own method. Not so Johnson's. Nor the free-verse line break, which has not been rationalized or bureaucratized. There is still no place for it in institutionalized punctuation (except where line breaks might as well not be line breaks, having been defused and quietly subsumed under the punctuational *system*). The free-verse line break is the unformulated space we have to maneuver in, to risk production in. The line break could be compared to what Althusser, in another context, called

a wild practice (*une pratique sauvage*) in the sense in which Freud spoke of a wild analysis, one which does not provide the theoretical credentials for its operations and which raises screams from the philosophy of the "interpretation" of the world.[18]

The difference is that line breaks exact screams not from "the philosophy of interpretation" but from the method of punctuation, or from the conceit that punctuation is simply a method, an organizational indifference, rather than an ideological function. The method of punctuation has positive aspects: it is socialized, a common medium that is thereby transmissible. But it also suppresses. The method is a content, after all, a function of values, which are always social values.[19] Relative to that method and its inscribed values, the line break is a freewheeling variable. It has the potential for being more than a social function or functionary. It may act, catalyze. It may become a practice. If punctuation were a deck of cards, each with an assigned value, the line break would be the joker in the pack.

6   line breaks as historically specific social practices

At best a poem is not a thing but a practice. A social practice. At the very least it is a social function. But any poem is socially conditioned, constituted and effected insofar as it is produced *by, about, through* and *for*. Line breaks, as poetic practice, threaten to rupture the ideological prophylaxis imposed on all production or potential production by routine behavior, routine 'perceptions' and routine 'truth.' Such line breaks are not boundaries but areas of engagement, of interaction between work and reader. They further enlist the reader as joint producer of the poem—not only the reader who exists after the fact, the historical reader, but the one inscribed in the text. So the reader is not an object of the text but a subject along with it (a socialized subject, not the liberally mandated "decentered" subject that has been assumed, bodily, into academic heaven).[20] Yet if certain poems, poetries and line breaks are social *practices,* what makes them such?

The Russian Formalists figured that the *dominanta* of poetry—what makes poetry poetry—is that it is written in lines. But going beyond dehistoricized formalistic concerns, others came to regard literature as a practice that "enacts a transformation of received categories of thought and expression" and that *"disorganizes* the forms through which the world is customarily perceived, opening up a kind of chink through which the world displays to view new and unexpected aspects." This disorganization was termed *ostranenie,* estrangement or defamiliarization. What literature defamiliarized was not only assumptions about language itself, but "certain dominant conceptions— ideologies...of the social world" (Bennett, [21]). Literature becomes, then, a site of ideological struggle, at least when it's a writing, a practice, rather than an exercise in stylistics. Such is the practice characterized by Brecht in his explanation of the A-effect (alienation effect): "The A-effect consists in turning the object of which one is to be made aware, to which one's attention is to be drawn, from something ordinary, familiar, immediately accessible, into something peculiar, striking and unexpected. What is obvious is in a certain sense made incomprehensible, but this is only in order that it may then be made all the easier to comprehend. Before familiarity can be turned into awareness the familiar must be stripped of its inconspicuousness; we must give up assuming that the object in question needs no explanation."[22]

Obviously there are layers and degrees of expectations and "estrangements." Line breaks disrupt and defamiliarize not only the dominant conceptions of the reader, say, but the poem's own hypothetically lineless, 'sentenced' discourse. As a practice, poetry works the way Schoenberg's music does, or did—music which Adorno says "demands from the very beginning active and concentrated participation, the most acute attention to simultaneous multiplicity, the renunciation of the customary crutches of a listening which always knows what to expect...It requires the reader spontaneously to compose its inner movement and demands of him not mere contemplation but praxis."[23] I would take this further. A realized work entails not simply textual or discourse praxis, but extratextual social praxis.

There are complications, especially regarding reception. A poetry that practices—that distances and defamiliarizes prevailing ideology, or that bores from within and abets the deconstruction of that ideology, in either case going beyond the pale of disciplinary 'culture' as defined and maintained by bourgeois institutions—may be perceived as formless. Responding to a poem of mine called "What is Poetry," a literature professor asked, in good faith, if I gave consideration to form. He meant any consideration, having assumed that as the work did not exhibit a form he was prepared to recognize, there was no formal concern. He was also assuming that 'form,' artistic form, ruled out certain contents, and that dissident political consciousness demanded poetic insensibility if not, necessarily, poetic ignorance. His ideological enclosure, ideological *suffusion,* allowed him to experience neither more nor less than his own expectation of what he *would* experience.

What had the poem done? Formally it mimicked, aurally mocked, what it challenged: bourgeois belles-lettres characterizations and definitions of poetry.[24] Each verse paragraph was governed by the title, the ambiguous question/ declaration "what is poetry."[25] The second one, singling out a New Critical fetish, read:

> or is it ironic, does it echo, echo what
> does it have ears

Presumably a reader trained in belles lettres would register the off-keyed consonant-and-vowel weave of *ironic / echo, echo / ears,* or the heavyhanded "echo, echo." Or might note—in verses of hearing, not hearing, and irony defined as echolalia—that the line ends on "what" (whaaat? cupped ear, or hearing horn). The issue is the bare existence and apprehensibility of formal concern, not quality or lack of it. Perhaps, given the ideological imperative to associate dissidence with formlessness (an association that scarcely veils its political bogeymen, the spectres of chaos, anarchy, barbarism), these verses may have a failing the Horatian Sapphics had. They may, like a dog whistle, be unhearable in the upper reaches of the animal kingdom.

Still there were more blatant formalities. The next verse paragraph, broaching other assumptions about poetry, commemorated a different stylistic:

> at night whom does it adore
> yet at dawn
> what dream would it go to the wall for

The three lines are all. Nonetheless the full rhymes, the alliterative decisiveness, the positing of grand passionate gestures, were to evoke the ballad quatrain in its later, romanticized form—at once rhythmically emphatic (adore, dawn, wall for) and aurally muzzy (whom, dawn, dream). Not that anyone might make such overly particularized associations, but it should be possible to detect evidence of formal consciousness, even as form is understood within the conventions of bourgeois belles lettres. Should be. But in this case it was not possible, because the disciplinary conventions regarding 'form' were, and are, overdetermined by silent, extradisciplinary ideological priorities. Those priorities were bound, when pressed, to exact their due. For the literature professor whose notion of form was so provincial and so deeply politicized as to seem universal and apolitical, any formal properties of the poem had been precluded by its political positioning. Though of course, as he presumed the matter, the reverse was true. As he saw it, the politics of the poem had made it oblivious of formal considerations. In any event, politics were clearly in command of his casual 'literary' question. What he was demonstrating, without intending to, is how easily formal training may be undone, *or put in its place,* by the very ideology that has been underwriting it.

The point is not those lines, though, nor someone's reading of them. I want only to indicate the ramifications of "mere technical" questions, and to raise the hidden agenda that shifts and may displace them. This is only the most obvious problem facing those who would *write,* who would produce a poetry that is a practice—a poetry that welcomes its condition as social practice and that would resist the glossing of prevailing ideology (which emanates always from the perspective, though not always necessarily from the persons, of those who wield social power). In the glare of work that is ideologically inadmissible, there's a conspicuous failure to recognize formal engagement. This alone gives the lie to the supposed autonomy of art and art-specific concerns. Clearly, although poetic technique is a function of poetic practice, poetic practice is itself subsumed under social practice. This is one of the many reasons why there can be no neat, unproblematical way to wrap up discussion of it.

7   two line breaks: social practice of and about language

The text is a six-line poem which as prose (or de-versed—it never did exist as prose) would read:

> They call the rage of the oppressed extremist. Evenhanded censure, from the hypothetical center of the slaughter, they call impartial, objective.

This airs a skepticism, and that's about it. If I volunteered that the second sentence 'quotes' Oscar Romero, the assassinated archbishop of San Salvador, even then one might at most *suspect* that the two sentences intend more meaning than they realize. Certainly more meaning than they enact. (Though if one has never heard of Oscar Romero, as most people have not, then the information may suggest nothing of the sort.) What the verse version of those sentences does, then, is attempt to realize that meaning. The poem is titled "Golden Mean," which by itself might refer simply to the prudent way, the course between extremes.

> They call the rage of the oppressed
> extremist.

> Evenhanded
> censure,
> from the hypothetical center of

> the slaughter, they call impartial, objective

Whereas the prose withheld a final disposition, the verse does not. It sides. Accuses. Yet that is still not the significant distinction between the two versions. The prose suggests, discreetly, that something is missing from the ethic of the golden mean, the reproachless middle way (in Latin, the *aurea mediocritas*).[26] But the verse risks more than the tepid irony of the unversed sentences. The question is what, and by what means does it do so. Within the sentence-meanings there are line-meanings. But the lines are escaping their sentences. At least, up to a point they are. Here the relationship between sentence and lines is more involved. The line-meaning—in particular the isolated final line, the bottom line—is *in one sense* no more than an extension of the sentence-meaning.[27] This is significant. Although the line-meaning goes so far that it seems to rupture the sentence-meaning, it nonetheless does not contradict the sentence but surfaces from within it.

To be specific. The second sentence, from "Evenhanded" to "objective," is payed out in four lines. Not in the usual way, however. The last line breaches the sentence itself. It's a kind of thought-caesura: *in* the sentence, but seemingly not *of* it. The prose sentence had implied the inadequacy of the golden mean; the line-broken version projects that immaculate ethic as the opposite of what it appears, and intends, to be. In the verse the golden mean acts in complicity with what it 'opposes.' Its *terms* of moderation are *enacted* as cover for, as medium for, criminal excess:

the slaughter, they call impartial, objective

Brecht once said that "moralists of this sort see man as existing for morality, not morality for man." He referred to ethics which dehistoricize and idealize themselves— abstracted ethics which, in their concrete historical being, directly contra*vene* their own idealist self-projections. This is not hypocrisy, which at least attests to an unproblematic or uncontested moral norm. This is a dissociation which masks its own content, even from itself.

In considering line breaks even as sheer physical phenomena (if that were possible) we have to take into account their integration into the aural weave reinforcing and 'pointing' them. This is as true of free verse as of prescribed verse. Rhyming or chiming that is opportunistic is not thereby purposeless. In one sense "Golden Mean" is an exegesis of the social use and the effective meaning of "objective," a word that under prevailing ideology has almost scriptural status. The aural signature of the word, notably the short emphatic *e* is the aural motif of the poem. It is central to most of the key words (oppressed, extremist, hypothetical center) and casually evident in the one other (evenhanded). That insistent, obtrusive note sets up "objective." Admittedly, this is possible because there are so few words. In a longer poem such details might be functionless minutiae.

The line breaking, like the presiding vowel, is tight-lipped. This has to do with timing, but the timing, in turn, is linked to correspondences and how they are apprehended. The first line break allows the conjunction of "oppressed" and "extremist" to sink in, to register *as* a conjunction. The line break thus exposes the unbroken sentence—the prose sentence that had tended, as ruling ideology tends, to make the linkage between enraged "oppressed" and "extremist" appear seamless, natural, covering over the fact that such linkage issues from the perspective of the oppressing system itself. The break exists to enhance or activate critical awareness of the shameless ideological transaction set out in, and papered over by, the first prose sentence. That sentence *as* sentence is one thing; broken open, it is a recounting and a posture, a position, vis-à-vis what is recounted. The next line/paragraph break seems to set forth alternatives:

extremist.

Evenhanded

What's more, the 'good guy' is capitalized. But aurally this second broken sentence (whose loaded predication, "call," reserved for the last line, quotes and turns the predication of the first sentence) starts to sound like the first one. Going from "extremist" to "censure" is like marking time in place. More deliberated still, the line break after "censure" is reinforced by a redundant comma, making this the most leaden of line breaks. It is a set-up for the following, tilting line we're slid to the far edge of:

from the hypothetical center of

of what, of

the slaughter,

which slaughter? the slaughter

they call impartial, objective

That slaughter... The penultimate line break has been a plotting function, an unsubtle peripety. The syntactical derangement of the conclusion—the last line read momentarily as itself, all by itself—is not only to give scrupulous definition to the golden mean in golden-mean terms, but to expose its historical content, its effective meaning.[28]

The point is not ironic. The issue is not hypocrisy. Those who say these things, who maintain these positions, say what they mean and mean what they say. What they say and mean is in fact what they do—except, the effective content of their saying is not what it seems. Not what it seems even to them. Evenhandedness, historically, is not evenhandedness. A golden-mean ethic assumes a position above and beyond what is assessed. Judgment issues *as though from outside* the historically specific terms of conflict and struggle. What this is, then, is a classic case of liberal moralism: golden, reproachless, *effectively* mean.[29] It disdains, as it facilitates, what is happening, no matter how terrible that may be, while presuming for itself the privilege of sanctuary. Sanctuary from history itself. Now all this is latent in the prose sentences, but only latent. The line breaking proposes to trouble the sentenced surface, to release ideologically suppressed meaning. The emergent meaning configuration of the bottom line enables the saying of what cannot be said (cannot be said not because it isn't true, but because it's outrageous): namely, that evenhanded censure neutralizes the slaughter, covers it up with a dehistoricized impartiality, and so abets it.

I'll conclude with another polemical example: "Taking Liberties," a poem that turns on the distinction between a historically specific conception of civil liberties and a dehistoricized one whereby "civil liberties" is maintained as a transcendent principle. (That the particular *definition* of civil liberties is class-specific, that it applies primarily to speech, is a peculiarity that the poem does not deal with.) The issue is framed by a quote attributed to Voltaire.[30] "I disapprove of what you say, but I'll defend to the death your right to say it."

TAKING LIBERTIES

Here it comes
quoting (sort of)
Voltaire

but Voltaire's
point was to let
misery speak, not
be tongue-tied
pieces on the rack

where was that
meaning lost?

this
one steps in: in
Greensboro Skokie
Salt Lake
City Decatur Chattanooga
Buffalo through

blood flaming crosses
firebombs,
untouched

this

ACLU
clears the way,
greases the rails
for Nazis, Klan, academic
fascists from Stanford, Berkeley, Harvard

stiff upper lip
screaming
"I may disagree with what they say

(they? what *do* they say?)
but I'll defend to the death
their right to say it"

and 'yes' we cry, yes of course
but
whose death

whose
death did you defend
their right to

really now

The poem goes through the quote (and the purpose it serves now) to the quite different social content of that quote in its historical context. Unlike those who believe that freedom of speech is to be upheld for its own sake, Voltaire's historically focused

point was to let
misery speak, not
be tongue-tied
pieces on the rack

The line breaks, and the consonantal clip, have a mimetic function:

point, speak, pieces
point, let, tongue-tied
speak, rack

They magnify the excruciating bind Voltaire addressed. (Whether I'm describing what the lines do or rationalizing them—though the distinction is itself problematical—is beside the point. What's at issue is how we conceive, and conceive of, the ways and means of technique.) Voltaire's was a subversive, liberating gesture. But after his point is detailed in the poem, the next two lines, visibly stranded, stir to the realization that something is missing between there and here, then and now. The 'original,' which is to say the historical, meaning is missing.

> where was that
> meaning lost?

Where was *Voltaire's* meaning lost? But also, insofar as we apprehend lines even as we read sentences, this says/asks *where* was that, and concludes (incredulous?)

> meaning lost?

Because meaning did lose, was lost, when Voltaire's 'quote' was spirited from the social relations it had been produced through and into. For him this was not an abstract principle. It was a means to *empower* the relatively powerless. However, his position, which literally *is* a position, has since been turned into a vacuous, dehistoricized piety.

Later in the poem, while Voltaire's sentiment is assented to, the historical exemption imposed on it ("I'll defend to the death / their right to say it" is frequently cited by civil libertarians who defend Nazis and the Klan) is challenged.

> and 'yes' we cry, yes of course
> but
> whose death
>
> whose
> death did you defend
> their right to
>
> really now

If civil liberties is decontextualized and reduced to 'free speech,' and if it does not flow from an overriding commitment to social justice—if the Voltairean posture is privileged as a principle in and of itself, regardless of the dispositions of power—it may and will serve social *injustice*. Speech may be powerful or powerless. The issue is not speech, but power. Power permits speech or disallows it. Yet even that is the least of it. More subtly, insidiously, power gives speech *meaning*. Social power can make 'Free World' a term and a category that includes Chile, Turkey, the West Bank, El Salvador, Honduras, South Africa, Northern Ireland, South Korea and the South Bronx. It can make bee feces 'chemical warfare' and make chemical warfare 'defoliation.' It can dissociate Agent Orange from 'yellow rain,' can grace Somoza's unredeemed butchers as 'freedom fighters,' and turn ketchup into a vegetable. With regard to Voltaire, then, the question is what does the despecified "defending to the death" translate into. What is its actual, effective meaning? How is it enacted now:

whose death

that is the question. Yet not a question. That death is not the death of the moralist or witness, the one whose survival is categorically *not* at stake. Even if taken at face value, the offer to "defend to the death" is at best an act of noblesse oblige, the charitable obligation of unconstrained will, the gesture of one superior to the conditions he or she chooses to intervene in. But of course the offer is not serious. Those who talk abstractly about sacrificing themselves for others are seldom the ones who do so. The evidence for this has long been in. That is why the text, which has been in the present, in its final predication shifts into the past tense, the done with:

whose
death did you defend
their right to

Not do, but did. Rather than impose the answering reality, the line break is meant to flash, as a rupture of the sentence, the concrete reality of this presumably Voltairean principle *when that principle is wielded as though it were above history*:

death did you defend

And this is no longer a question. The locution of the line, the line apprehended itself and not simply as subsumed by the sentence, is archaic, pondered. It cannot be mistaken for ironic. At least, I don't believe it can. It is humorless, unlike the talky close: *really now.* Meaning not as fancied, not in no-time, but really, and now. In sum, the sentence has been broken to release meaning—the suppressed meaning inscribed within the sentence, and the meaning of the quote that has (had) been deracinated, deprived of its life source.

This says nothing about the quality of the poem, its success or its failure. Again, my comments are intended only to indicate a way of thinking about technique. Technique not as a skill, simply, but as a practice. I've selected two line breaks produced as polemical, demystifying practices. They are not the only kinds of line breaks, not even in the works cited. But they are, on the face of it, the least defensible in terms of bourgeois belles lettres, philosophy, morality. Other line breaks serve other functions and constitute other practices. The point is that line breaking, like writing itself, *is* a practice.[31] And however much it may be a poetic practice (or an ad or graffiti practice), it is unavoidably a social practice. Further, only *as* social practice does it have "meaning." Questions of value, the evidence shows, are also historically conditioned. Not determined, necessarily, but conditioned. That means socially conditioned. And, where there are classes, class-conditioned.

The ramifications go on. In writing to demystify bourgeois ideology, yet doing so in terms of bourgeois belles lettres, I write within a convention available to a tiny portion of the bourgeoisie itself. This convention effectively precludes participation by the vast majority of people—whose needs it does not meet, does not comprehend, and in fact hardly addresses. Although I, along with others, may propose to write for the countless number who literally or effectively cannot read this, I write to those whose language I use—those who with few exceptions will not want to read this (not only because it demands of them time and energy, but also because it shrugs off, attacks or occasionally dismantles their own verities), or who will apprehend it in terms of the social understanding, the ideology, that constitutes the restricted purview of their 'aesthetic' values. This is not a circumstance to be regretted or moralized on. It is what the specific historical situation, including my place in it, allows. The writing, with its contradictions, is conditioned on that situation. At most, that writing is an act of resistance, a struggle. But the overcoming of these contradictions would require, among other things, a redisposition of social power: not the spreading of bourgeois belles lettres to masses of people (a missionary presumption that could only serve to extend bourgeois hegemony, especially if power relationships remained unchanged), but the development of forms, ways of apprehending, that correspond to *and enable* the empowerment of the disfranchised. Without the conditions for such a poetry, or culture, there is no way of producing it. No one knows what that poetry would be like, or even if the term 'poetry' would be retained. That might or might not matter. "The time will come," wrote Wallace Stevens in his *Adagia*, "when poems like Paradise will seem like very *triste* contraptions."[32] The category 'poetry' could become something of a dead language, perhaps one with residual attraction, like "masque" or "madrigal." Or not. It might survive, yet be as distinct from the poetry of bourgeois belles lettres as the powerfully impacted painting of Masaccio is distinct from the iconic stillness of Duccio, each of which epitomized its historical moment, both in what it expressed and what repressed.

The social practice of the two poems cited above tries to be, given its limitations, a challenge to bourgeois belles lettres. It insists on the extra-aesthetic values inscribed in the bourgeois aesthetic.[33] And it looks forward to the outgrowing or overthrowing of those exclusive, historically provincial terms. This can't be accomplished by fiat, nor by sheer willpower, nor by manipulating a language deprived of social power and accountability. It will take a social recasting, in effect a revolution. Not a metaphorical one.

The subject here is, and has been, language. The immediate project—the one I've been concerned with, that informs the way I conceive line breaks—is to demystify current language. To gauge its historically specific gravity. To figure what it enacts, in order to act through it and on it, or at least to avoid becoming a functionary of the ideology inscribed in it. The basic assumption has been that a fully realized poetry consists not of stylistics but of writing. That poetry is a practice. And that, it follows, a fully realized poetry will also be a kind of antipoetry.

1   Pierre Macherey, A *Theory of Literary Production*, (London: Routledge and Kegan Paul, 1978), 100.

2   In a retrospective lecture given in 1954, Siqueiros, the Mexican painter and muralist, raised a historically specific instance of this: "From the time of Odilon Redon there was talk in France of 'art for art's sake,' of pure art, which would totally eliminate from art the image of both man and things…This was the beginning of an art which was purely geometrical, a play of forms and colors, a simple organization of shades; anything that might explain man's existence and his problems was excluded. It was logical that they next declared: 'Art has no connection with social problems…' I would like to ask, when has art

not been committed? Was Christian art not committed?...There is a lot of speculation today about what people call the abstract forms of pre-Hispanic art in Mexico. There is nothing abstract anywhere in Meso-American art. The ancient Mexicans used their art to create a specific language, hieroglyphics. What we today see as abstract forms were letters for them, letters with a brilliant plastic quality but they were letters, slogans, prayers, historical facts, scientific explanations. There is not a single thing in the whole of pre-Hispanic painting and sculpture...which is exclusively decorative or purely abstract. Many artists of today borrow elements from pre-Hispanic arts; but they only take the shell, they cannot take the kernel, and they forget that the shell was the result of the kernel, i.e. of the ideological function which art had at that time." David A. Siqueiros, *Art and Revolution* (London: Lawrence and Wishart, 1975), 158.

3   Andrei Voznesensky, *Antiworlds and "The Fifth Ace,"* Patricia Blake and Max Hayward, eds. (New York: Doubleday Anchor, 1967), 89.

4   This does not apply exclusively to bourgeois academic criticism. Most leftist literary criticism in the U.S. also observes the niceties of bourgeois belles lettres. It is a criticism that cannot or dares not theorize itself. But then most 'Marxist' literary theory doesn't risk much either. Class analysis, and working class partisanship, are given short shrift or simply dissolved. There's a reluctance to *practice*. It's as though, in the domain of literature, the historic enterprise to transform social reality has been abandoned. Edward Said, questioning the disabling limitations he believes have been accepted by Jameson and Eagleton among others, has called for "us" to break out "of the disciplinary ghettos in which we as intellectuals have been confined" and "to consider that the audience for literacy is not a closed circle of three thousand professional critics but the community of human beings living in society." Edward Said, "Opponents, Audiences, Constituencies and Communities," *The Anti-Aesthetic: Essays on Postmodern Culture,* Hal Foster, ed. (Seattle, Wash.: Bay Press, 1983), 158.

5   In *The Politics of Education: Culture, Power and Liberation,* Paulo Freire claims that "insofar as language is impossible without thought, and language and thought are impossible without the world to which they refer, the human word is more than mere vocabulary—it is word-and-action. The cognitive dimensions of the literacy process must include the relationships of men with their world...Learning to read and write ought to be an opportunity for men to know what *speaking the word* really means: a human act implying reflection and action. As such it is a primordial right and not the privilege of a few. Speaking the word is not a true act if it is not at the same time associated with the right of self-expression and world-expression, of creating and re-

creating, of deciding and choosing and ultimately participating in society's historical process" (p. 50).

6 The poetry of the Parnassians and the prose poems of Rimbaud are not mere sites of poetic exchange. Much might be made of Parnassian strategy and characteristics in the context of the Second Empire, a period of reaction, and much *has* been made of Rimbaud's disturbing experience of the Paris Commune of 1871, an event that disrupted the understandings of the Second Empire.

7 Michael Davidson, "Writing at the Boundaries," *New York Times Book Review,* 24 February 1985, p. 1.

8 Davidson is making a case for what is sometimes called "language poetry." A few Marxist critics do the same. We may respond to this with Marx and Engels's critique of the Young Hegelians (especially if for "consciousness" we substitute "language"). In *The German Ideology* (New York: International Publishers, 1947) they write: "Since, according to their fantasy, the relationships of men, all their doings, their chains and their limitations are products of their consciousness, the Young Hegelians'…demand to change consciousness amounts to a demand to interpret reality in another way, i.e. to recognize it by means of another interpretation. The Young Hegelian ideologists, in spite of their allegedly 'world-shattering' statements, are the staunchest conservatives. The most recent of them have found the correct expression for their activity when they declare they are only fighting against '*phrases.*' They forget, however, that to these phrases they themselves are only opposing other phrases, and that they are in no way combating the real existing world when they are merely combating the phrases of this world" (p. 41).

9 We might conjecture as to the formative circumstances of Chinese letter poems. Most poets, especially as clerks, lived displaced lives in a land of great and dangerous distances, during unsettled times, working in the administration of one or another warlord. Certainly that was the case with Tu Fu. Letter poems seem to have been communications among chronically separated friends and family members. By way of contrast, consider Coleridge's decision to turn his "Dejection" verse letter, written to Sarah Hutchinson, and much preoccupied with complaints about his own domestic life, into the familiar "Dejection: An Ode." The original, while not always attractive, does generate an uneasy power. The expurgated version huffs and puffs, making much ado. For obvious personal reasons, Coleridge had to uproot the verse letter, removing it from specific grounds. Even so, for 'poetic' reasons alone it's unlikely he could have kept it as is—not having an available model, such as the Chinese provides, that would allow the verse letter to be credited *as* a poem. (Which may also be

why "Kubla Khan" could be presented only as the fragment of a poem, one wrapped in explanation, apology and disclaimer. Coleridge was stuck. Surely the poem felt right to him, but what available notion of 'poem' did it correspond to?) Of course there is, or was, a tradition of English letter poems. Such poems have been based mostly on Horatian models (directly or indirectly, e.g., Ben Jonson's "Inviting a Friend to Supper," or Wyatt's "Mine Own John Poins," which came to him through Luigi Alamanni, a contemporary Italian poet). Yet these are actually see-through letters, and what we see through them, as through the epistles of Horace, are conversational essays: social *performances* rather than intimate communications.

10 *The Odes of Horace,* James Michie, trans. (New York: Washington Square Press, 1965), 229.

11 Peter Bürger, in *Theory of the Avant-Garde* (Minneapolis: University of Minnesota Press, 1984), holds that the avant-garde negates aestheticism and "the autonomy of art." He claims that Breton's automatic texts "should be read as guides to individual production," and that production should not be understood as artistic production simply but "as part of a liberating life praxis. That is what is meant by Breton's demand that poetry be practiced (*pratiquer la poésie*)" (p. 53). That may be so, though the evidence in Breton's case is less than convincing. Mayakovsky and the Russian Futurists are a more compelling instance of an avant-garde that really did struggle to become "a liberating life praxis," in particular because they did so not only on behalf of an elite.

Bürger does though have a useful critique of artistic autonomy. "To summarize: the *autonomy of art* is a category of bourgeois society. It permits the description of art's detachment from the context of practical life as a historical development—that among the members of those classes which, at least at times, are free from the pressures of the need for survival, a sensuousness could evolve that was not part of any means-ends relationships. Here we find the moment of truth…What this category cannot lay hold of is that this detachment of art from practical contexts is a *historical process*, i.e., that it is socially conditioned. And here lies the untruth of the category, the element of distortion that characterizes every ideology…The category 'autonomy' does not permit the understanding of its referent as one that developed historically. The relative dissociation of the work of art from the praxis of life in bourgeois society thus becomes transformed into the (erroneous) idea that the work of art is totally independent of society" (p. 46).

12 To turn a phrase from Althusser, discussions of technique in "the language of technique" are submissions to the "game" which constitutes technique *as* technique, i.e., as autonomous.

13 All descriptions are historically specific appropriations and reconstitutions. See Freud's 1914 essay, "The Moses of Michelangelo," which recounts descriptions and interpretations of Michelangelo's remarkable sculpture (Moses has "horns" on his head), and of the ways in which descriptions are skewed by interpretations projected *through* them onto the sculpture itself.

Another accessible documentation of historically conditioned appropriations and reconstitutions is Albert Fried's *John Brown's Journey* (New York: Anchor/Doubleday, 1978), which retraces not only Brown's life, or rather his political life's journey as sifted through the author's own, but the journey of Brown's "image" as it passed through the times, understandings and politics of various historians writing about Brown. This is a process we're aware of, but that abstracted awareness has yet to be incorporated in our productions and analyses.

14 To demonstrate how misleading and reductive the 'end-stopped'/'run-on' opposition is, we need only look at actual line breaks. To touch on just a few, mostly from Wordsworth...

Some run-on lines function as run-ons are supposed to function:

> And all the shadowy banks on either side
> Came sweeping through the darkness...

Yet other run-ons are *more* so. Lacking the definite article that would 'nominalize' and thereby stabilize the adjective "gray," the third line of Yeats's "Easter 1916" doesn't so much run on, but collapses, into the line following:

> I have met them at close of day
> Coming with vivid faces
> From counter or desk among gray
> Eighteenth century houses.

Still other run-ons read as, have the feel of, end-stopped lines. We experience them as end-stopped—until, having arrived at the succeeding line, we apprehend them retrospectively (experience them retroactively?) as run-on:

> ...while far distant hills
> Into the tumult sent an alien sound
> Of melancholy not unnoticed...

The line had seemed self-sufficient, and that seeming had allowed the following line, a syntactic continuation, to slip quietly in under the voiding of our expectations. We don't get other than what we expect, but in the place of no-expectation we find ourselves in the welling presence of melancholy—delicately introduced by the reticent line break, then trailing in at the hand of an affirming double negative (*"not un*noticed"). That there is no conventional punctuation after "sound" is irrelevant. The feeling of rightness, of sufficiency or closure, comes more from syntax than from punctuation as such. There are even run-on lines, such as those relating the windblown, water-carrying girl in Book XII of *The Prelude,* which seem to *impede* forward-reading progress.

15 The contradiction between the socialization of memory and the private appropriation of it (indirectly, through government agency, and directly, by banks and other corporations with the resources to create and/or buy their way into information storage systems) corresponds to the contradiction between the social character of production and the private ownership of the means of production.

16 See "The Rise of English" in Terry Eagleton's *Literary Theory: An Introduction* (Minneapolis: University of Minnesota Press, 1983) and Brian Doyle's "The Hidden History of English Studies," along with essays by others, in *Re-Reading English* (London: Methuen, 1982), Peter Widdowson, ed.

It should be noted, however, that U. S. owners of production have had to accelerate the development of cheaper labor (in effect, the development of more and more reducible and interchangeable units of labor). This has increased as well their need to maintain social equilibrium. Which is to say, social silence. Paradoxically, yet not paradoxically, this project has been served by increased *illiteracy.* According to Alan Finder in *The New York Times* (3 January 1985), "more than 26 million English-speaking Americans are functionally illiterate, unable to write a check, address an envelope or read a notice in a store…Another 46 million cannot read proficiently" (p. CI). That is nearly a third of the population. Yet illiteracy does not occur naturally. It is socially created. At present, with a highly integrated *and* fragmented labor force, and domestically with service industries overtaking industrial production, and with labor "units" becoming more and more interchangeable and therefore replaceable—a speed-up of the process examined in Harry Braverman's *Labor and Monopoly Capital*—there is yet more systemic pressure to 'thingify' and devalue *individual* labor.

It may not be coincidental that the production of illiteracy corresponds, functionally, to the intensification of academic disciplines. Increasing specialization increases social/intellectual stupefaction. Under the appearance of producing knowledge it produces ignorance; all it 'learns' is its own terms. Disciplines become a disability: an inability to *read* the world and one's actual relations with it. Become, in short, another illiteracy.

17   For a detailed, historically specific account of the ideologically significant conflict between theorized and untheorized punctuation (though he doesn't use these terms), see Barry Menikoff's *Robert Louis Stevenson and 'The Beach of Falesá,': A Study in Victorian Publishing with the Original Text* (Stanford: Stanford University Press, 1984), 32-57.

18   The "philosophy of the 'interpretation' of the world" is distinguished from the philosophy of the transformation of the world, i.e., Marxism, which Gramsci termed "the philosophy of praxis." Perhaps what most disturbs the philosophy of interpretation (bourgeois philosophy) is that the philosophy of praxis demands a radical relocation of epistemology. It is not only, as Marx has it in his eleventh thesis on Feuerbach, that "the philosophers have only *interpreted* the world, in various ways; the point however is to *change* it." That might still leave bourgeois philosophy intact, an object rather than a subject of practice. But to link knowledge with practice—to realize that knowledge not only depends on social practice but is constituted by it—threatens the philosophy of interpretation, of ahistorical 'mind,' spectatorial 'objectivity' and the like.

19   The method of punctuation is as much social content as is the seemingly neutral cut of a business suit—which John Berger analyzes as an idealization of sedentary, nonmanual power. See "The Suit and the Photograph," an essay on the photographs of August Sander, in *About Looking* (New York: Pantheon, 1980).

20   It is possible to speak of a "decentered subject" only in analysis, not in practice or production. The "decentered subject" only confirms the liberal philosophical dissociation of thinking from doing. It is a parodic version of the circumstance that any "subject" is necessarily socialized. (This is conveniently articulated if we transpose Yerkes's formulation, "one chimpanzee is no chimpanzee," to read "one human being is no human being.") As subjects we do not exist as metaphysical entities but are linguistically constituted in discourse and, more profoundly, socially constituted in and through history. What allows for change, and for the subject to be an agent of change, is that the discourse and the history consist of, and generate, internal contradictions, the terms of which are always in motion, and are themselves unfixed.

21   Tony Bennett, *Formalism and Marxism* (New York: Methuen, 1979), 24.

22   John Willett, ed., *Brecht on Theatre* (New York: Hill and Wang, 1964), 143-144. Of course any literature is an ideologically saturated site. Only literature-as-stylistics is ideologically implicated, however. *That*

literature merely "acts as a privileged region of ideology within which, by concealing its contradictions as they manifest themselves at the level of language, the whole system of dominant ideology is reproduced, preserved intact as an ongoing system in spite of the tensions with which it is racked" (Bennett, pp.161-162).

23 Theodor Adorno, *Prisons* (Cambridge, Mass.: MIT Press, 1981),149-150.

24 The term "bourgeois belles lettres" is descriptive. It is not an expression of disdain. The simple fact is that what are designated 'culture' and 'literature' are neither produced nor experienced by the vast majority of people. Here and now the inscribed perspectives and values of literature are classbound. We don't have to read the quarterlies or the *New York Times Book Review* to figure out that literature, as we know it, is a property of the bourgeoisie. Literature is a historical, not an aesthetic, category. The power to honor writings as 'literature' is exercised by the class that wields social power, which controls the production of 'education,' books, public ideas, etc. That control is not simply an effect of class domination but an instrument of it. As Gramsci noted through his concept of hegemony, "the rule of one class over another does not depend on economic or physical power alone but rather on persuading the ruled to accept the system of beliefs of the ruling class and to share its social, cultural and moral values" (summarized by James Joll in *Antonio Gramsci* [New York: Penguin, 1978], p.16). Whatever may constitute bourgeois belles lettres, its definitive feature does not have to do with what it is about, but what place it occupies and, even more so, what it is and is not doing. It is to be defined, then, less by its forms or abstracted ideas or dehistoricized principles than by its practices.

25 This and the following quotes are from *Apollo Helmet* (Willimantic, Conn.: Curbstone Press, 1983), a collection of poems bearing on poetry and public language.

26 From Horace, *Odes* II,x,5. Horace does not promote the golden mean as a positionless principle, however, or as a spectatorial ethic outside the conditions of actual life. For him it is a guide in and through life: a cultivation of life in the midst of life, not a superior's imposition on it. In the old, ringing translation by William Cowper:

> He that holds fast the golden mean,
> And lives contentedly between
> The little and the great,
> Feels not the wants that pinch the poor,
> Nor plagues that haunt the rich man's door,
> Embittering all his state.

27   Cf. Marianne Moore's poem, "The Steeple-Jack," the first line of which
reads:

Dürer would have seen a reason for living

before the sentence descends and renews itself in the anticlimactic,
but *not* anticlimactic, second line which clarifies:

in a town like this....

28   Cf. Thoreau on John Brown and Brown's critics: "*It was the fact that
the tyrant must give place to him or he to the tyrant that distinguished
him from all the reformers of the day that I know...*It was his peculiar
doctrine that a man has a perfect right to interfere by force with the
slaveholder, in order to rescue the slave. I agree with him. They who
are continually shocked by slavery have some right to be shocked by
the violent death of the slaveholder, but no others. Such will be more
shocked by the life than by his death. I shall not be forward to think
him mistaken in his method who quickest succeeds to liberate the
slave. *I speak for the slave when I say that I prefer the philanthropy of
Captain Brown to that philanthropy which neither shoots me nor
liberates me.*" Henry David Thoreau, "A Plea for Captain John Brown"
(30 October 1859), reprinted in *Anti-Slavery and Reform Papers*
(London: Swan and Sonnenschien, 1890), 74. The compatibility of
the evenhanded censure with the slaughter, the fact that neither must
"give place" to the other, renders that censure anything but impartial
or morally objective.

29   As Merleau-Ponty puts it: "The purity of principles not only tolerates
but even requires violence. Thus there is a mystification in liberalism.
Judging from history and by everyday events, liberal ideas belong to a
system of violence of which, as Marx said, they are the 'spiritual *point
d'honneur*,' the 'solemn complement' and the 'general basis of
consolation and justification'...Whatever one's philosophical or even
theological position, a society is not the temple of idol-values that
figure on the front of its monuments or in its constitutional scrolls;
the value of a society is the value it places upon man's relation to
man...To understand and judge a society, one has to penetrate its
basic structure to the human bond upon which it is built; this
undoubtedly depends upon legal relations, but also upon forms of
labor, ways of loving, living and dying...Principles and the inner life
are alibis the moment they cease to animate external and everyday
life...Any serious discussion of communism...will not brandish
liberal principles in order to topple communism; it will examine
whether it is doing anything to resolve the problem rightly raised by
communism, namely, to establish among men relations that are

human." Maurice Merleau-Ponty, *Humanism and Terror* (Boston: Beacon Press, 1969), xiii-xv.

30   The title, "Taking Liberties," refers to the taking away of civil liberties, of life as well as of speech, but also to liberties taken with Voltaire's intent as it would follow from his context, and, a bit pedantically, to the liberty taken in assigning the actual quote to him.

31   I do not wish to fetishize line breaks. Paragraph breaks and sentence breaks (whatever a sentence is) may also work as "wild practices." Or otherwise conventional punctuation, for instance a number of Emily Dickinson's internal dashes. Or parts of speech, conjunctions, say (I recall reading somewhere Hemingway's startlingly vicious sentence delivered on Gertrude Stein: "She was always very friendly, and for a long time she was affectionate").

32   Wallace Stevens, *Opus Posthumous* (London: Faber and Faber, 1959), 167.

33   However, the poems do attempt to negate the transcendental subject, the centerpiece of bourgeois ideology: the metaphysical notion of the individual as the undividable, of identity as entity. The materially conceived subject is more accurately conceived as a nexus in the web of social relations. A *socialized* subject. In "Golden Mean" the transcendental subject is negated; none is inserted or posited *within the understanding* of the poem. But stuck in the text, as undigestible as stone, the "they" not only conceives itself as a transcendental subject, but thereby *necessarily* posits another such, the "oppressed." As though the two were distinct entities. What the positing of those transcendental subjects suppresses is the realization of the socialized subject—which is, as well, the realization that the "they" and the "oppressed" are not self-contained entities but interdependent functions of one another (are contradictions *within* the comprehensive socialized subject).

James Scully, born 1937 in New Haven, CT, is a Professor Emeritus of the University of Connecticut, where he taught for many years in the English Department. He has won numerous honors for his creative work, including a Lamont Award and a Guggenheim Fellowship. He was the founding editor of Curbstone's "Art on the Line" series and has published nine books of poetry, three works in translation, and two works of criticism. His work appears in numerous anthologies.

He and his family spent 1973-1974 in Santiago de Chile, during the early stage of the Pinochet regime, which he documented in his poetry book, *Santiago Poems* (1975)—the first book Curbstone published and which served as an impetus for founding the Press.

Recently he has turned his hand to drama. In 1995, the Collective Artists at the Music Theatre and Opera Company in New York gave a staged reading of his play *About the Ironing Board*. In 2000, the American Theatre of Actors in New York produced his *Stepping Out*.

At present he lives in San Francisco.

CURBSTONE PRESS, INC.

is a non-profit publishing house dedicated to literature that reflects a
commitment to social change, with an emphasis on contemporary writing
from Latino, Latin American and Vietnamese cultures. Curbstone presents
writers who give voice to the unheard in a language that goes beyond
denunciation to celebrate, honor and teach. Curbstone builds bridges
between its writers and the public – from inner-city to rural areas, colleges to
community centers, children to adults. Curbstone seeks out the highest
aesthetic expression of the dedication to human rights and intercultural
understanding: poetry, testimonies, novels, stories,
and children's books.

This mission requires more than just producing books. It requires ensuring
that as many people as possible learn about these books and read them. To
achieve this, a large portion of Curbstone's schedule is dedicated to
arranging tours and programs for its authors, working with public school
and university teachers to enrich curricula, reaching out to underserved
audiences by donating books and conducting readings and community
programs, and promoting discussion in the media. It is only through these
combined efforts that literature can truly make a difference.

Curbstone Press, like all non-profit presses, depends on the support of
individuals, foundations, and government agencies to bring you, the reader,
works of literary merit and social significance which might not find a place
in profit-driven publishing channels, and to bring the authors and their
books into communities across the country. Our sincere thanks to the many
individuals, foundations, and government agencies who have recently
supported this endeavor: Community Foundation of Northeast Connecticut,
Connecticut Commission on Culture & Tourism, Connecticut Humanities
Council, Greater Hartford Arts Council, Hartford Courant Foundation,
Lannan Foundation, National Endowment for the Arts, and the
United Way of the Capital Area.

Please help to support Curbstone's efforts to present the diverse voices and
views that make our culture richer. Tax-deductible donations can be made
by check or credit card to:
Curbstone Press, 321 Jackson Street, Willimantic, CT 06226
phone: (860) 423-5110   fax: (860) 423-9242
www.curbstone.org

IF YOU WOULD LIKE TO BE A MAJOR SPONSOR OF A
CURBSTONE BOOK, PLEASE CONTACT US.